"In *Love Does Not Conquer A*
and practical advice offers a re
that every parent and child co
Tori Hope Pete

"*Love Does Not Conquer All* cuts straight to the heart of what it truly means to love children through the highs and lows of foster care and adoption. This book is a powerful testament to the resilience of both children and parents as they navigate the hidden scars and unexpected challenges that love alone cannot erase. As a foster and adoptive mom, I know firsthand that love is powerful but not always enough to heal deep wounds on its own. Peter's raw honesty and hard-earned wisdom bring hope and clarity to a journey that is as heartbreaking as it is rewarding. This book is a lifeline for parents and a guide to fostering with both heart and resilience."

Jen Lilley, actress, producer, and foster and adoptive mom

"In *Love Does Not Conquer All*, Peter Mutabazi offers a powerful and transformative guide for parents, drawing from the depths of his own tumultuous childhood. Now a devoted single Black father, Mutabazi weaves his personal narrative with his extensive experience raising over forty foster and adoptive children into an invaluable resource for those navigating their own intricate challenges of foster care and adoption. With raw honesty, transparency, and heartfelt reflections, he offers profound insights that should resonate deeply with anyone invested in the well-being of children. This compelling, thought-provoking, and child-centered book serves not only as a crucial resource for adoption agencies and child welfare professionals but also as essential reading for all parents striving to create loving and trauma-informed environments."

Rhonda M. Roorda, award-winning author of *In Their Voices: Black Americans on Transracial Adoption* and consultant to the Emmy Award-winning series *This Is Us*

"This book is a story of triumph—where Peter came from and where he has arrived as a parent is remarkable. We all have challenges as children, whether fostered, adopted, or birthed, but Peter's journey with his children is one of pure inspiration that can reach out to anyone, no matter your race or creed!"

Ruvé and Neal McDonough, producer and actors

"Peter Mutabazi has written an incredible expression of love and humor. His understanding of the hearts of children in the foster care system and his wisdom for fostering families is a rare gem. In this book, he offers realistic expectations, but he ends with hope for the journey for those who care for hurting and vulnerable children."

Tamalani Barnett, cofounder and executive
director of RaisingHOPE

"As a fellow foster/adoptive parent, I deeply appreciate Peter's insight and raw honesty. I pray this book inspires every reader to search their heart and ask how they can serve foster children and families. These children deserve our best, and Peter is proof that together we can change lives!"

Sara Arn, certified Arizona foster parent
trainer and adoptive mother of seven

"It's easy to stand on the sidelines and complain; as a society, we often spend more time talking than doing. Peter Mutabazi, however, is a man of action—a true example of service and compassion. Having survived a difficult life in Uganda, he now dedicates himself to serving God through adoption and foster care, embodying the hands and feet of Jesus. A must-read, *Love Does Not Conquer All* reminds us that life isn't like Hollywood: the foster care journey can be challenging, but God is with us every step of the way."

Bob Hamer, veteran undercover FBI agent and
author of *The Last Undercover*

"Peter's unconventional path to parenthood and the honest lessons he shares are profoundly inspiring for any parent. His relatable vulnerability shines as he navigates a world unfamiliar to many: foster care. Offering a rare and unflinching glimpse into the lives of teens in the system—often overlooked or misunderstood—he reveals the critical need for these children to be seen, loved, and parented. Peter's story reminds us that what may seem 'abnormal' is the norm for kids who have endured trauma. He challenges us to pause our judgments and truly witness the extraordinary transformations made possible through consistency, compassion, and an unwavering commitment of 'I will not leave you.'"

Nicole Taylor, chief communications and community
officer, Riverstone Logistics

LOVE DOES NOT CONQUER ALL

PREVIOUS BOOKS

Now I Am Known

LOVE

DOES NOT CONQUER ALL

And Other Surprising Lessons
I Learned as a Foster Dad to
MORE THAN 40 KIDS

PETER MUTABAZI

with Mark Tabb

BakerBooks

a division of Baker Publishing Group
Grand Rapids, Michigan

Published by Baker Books
a division of Baker Publishing Group
Grand Rapids, Michigan
BakerBooks.com

Printed in the United States of America

Library of Congress Cataloging-in-Publication Data
Names: Mutabazi, Peter, author. | Tabb, Mark A., author.
Title: Love does not conquer all : and other surprising lessons I learned as a foster dad to more than 40 kids / Peter Mutabazi, with Mark Tabb.
Description: Grand Rapids, Michigan : Baker Books, a division of Baker Publishing Group, [2025]
Identifiers: LCCN 2024051222 | ISBN 9781540904799 (paperback) | ISBN 9781540904973 (casebound) | ISBN 9781493450442 (ebook)
Subjects: LCSH: Foster parents. | Foster home care. | Parent and child. | Foster parents—Religious life. | Foster home care—Religious aspects—Christianity.
Classification: LCC HQ759.7 .M87 2025 | DDC 306.874—dc23/eng/20250117
LC record available at https://lccn.loc.gov/2024051222

Baker Publishing Group publications use paper produced from sustainable forestry practices and postconsumer waste whenever possible.

25 26 27 28 29 30 31   7 6 5 4 3 2 1

CONTENTS

SECTION 3

LESSONS SPECIFICALLY FOR FOSTER AND ADOPTIVE PARENTS

PROLOGUE

When we sign up to become parents, we volunteer for a lifelong job we can never fully master. Every day, we face new surprises we have to figure out on the fly. For those of us who like to plan out everything in advance and control whatever situation in which we may find ourselves, good luck. Mike Tyson once said everyone has a plan until they get punched in the mouth. For parents, something punches us in the mouth every day, and not just figuratively. The first blow usually comes within the first few hours of bringing a child home. Whether we are a bio parent or a foster or adoptive parent, we always think we know what to expect. For me, I went through hours upon hours of training to get my foster care license. I thought I knew what I was getting myself into. Then my first placement walked through the door, a five-year-old boy named Kaine.[1] Little did I realize that when it comes to parenting, you really have no idea of what you are getting yourself into until the kid walks through the door.

Over forty foster children and three adoptions later, I still find myself surprised on a daily basis. I never expected to have a child paint the bathroom with poop or destroy a school classroom or to find eight- and nine-year-olds making out like they

1. All children's names have been changed to protect their privacy.

saw people do in the homes from which they were removed. No one told me that one day I'd walk into my kitchen and find a child sitting on the counter completely naked, nor did I expect to find my next-door neighbor's video game console in my living room after one of my kids decided to rehome it without permission—i.e., they stole it. Yet I have discovered the surprises of parenting are also opportunities to learn and to grow as a human being and a dad. Most of the lessons I've picked up through my parenting journey I did not learn the first time I faced a surprising situation. That is also the beauty of being a dad. The surprises we encounter usually repeat themselves, which gives us a second and third and fourth and fifth and more chances to figure out how to best handle the situation.

I do not claim to be a parenting expert. None of my degrees are in early childhood development or psychology, although I have devoured everything I can on both topics both in preparing to become a dad and since as I've scrambled to find answers to behaviors that defy explanation. The book you hold in your hand was birthed through my experiences as a single dad who has had to be both father and mother to anywhere from three to seven children at a time. Much of what I write was also shaped by many, many conversations with other parents, especially other foster and adoptive parents. My collaborator on this project, Mark Tabb, with whom I also worked on my first book, *Now I Am Known*, is also an adoptive dad. His two youngest of five daughters came to live with Mark and his wife when they were thirteen and fifteen. Many of Mark's experiences mirror mine. His youngest daughters are now in their late twenties, which means he has lived through the phase of parenting I am just beginning with my oldest children. While the stories in this book are all mine, Mark's experiences can be felt throughout. I have also consulted with Marissa Bradford, a Harvard-educated child development specialist, during the writing of this book. She contributed several insights that can be found in many of the practical applications for parents.

When I first started writing this book, I envisioned it to be a key resource for foster and adoptive parents. However, one of our editors, Stephanie Smith, who has two young children, told us how the lessons in this book helped her understand and parent her bio children and encouraged me to broaden my vision. Her advice made this a much better book.

However your children have come into your home, through foster care or adoption or by birth, I pray what follows will give you hope in your parenting journey. My heart goes out to every parent. We all face a difficult road, but together, we can make it.

1

A Parenting Book from Who?

I am surprised Oklahoma Child Protective Services (CPS) placed children in my home. In preparation, I completed all the foster parent training classes, passed my home study and all the background checks, and did everything else required to get my foster care license. I also went to seminars and read everything I could get my hands on, especially the works of Karyn Purvis, author of *The Connected Child*. Reading that book, I felt like Purvis had looked back over my own childhood and given me strategies not only for my future children but also to help me heal from my past trauma. I also devised a little test for myself, to see how prepared I was to be a dad: I bought some of the most difficult houseplants to keep alive and set them up in my home. I figured that if I could keep those plants green, I was ready for a child.

However, no one had ever asked me *the* question that would have shown I lacked the one essential skill every parent of young children must have: "Do you know how to make the blue box mac and cheese?"

Blue box mac and cheese? Are you kidding? I don't eat dairy, and I definitely do not eat mac and cheese from a box, much less make it. If this news had gotten out, someone from CPS would have revoked my foster care license and banned me from having any children in my home. "You can't make mac and cheese?" my social worker would have said to me. "Your children will starve to death." I certainly never would have had any children placed in my home if I had gone on to explain that my children would have plenty to eat in my home because I could stir-fry a delicious skillet of any vegetable my kid might want. I now know a child would rather starve to death than eat cooked vegetables.

I also had no grasp on other key essentials for successful parenting. Before I became a dad, I did not realize that all chicken nuggets are not alike. I once made the mistake of serving my children nuggets from Chick-fil-A rather than McDonald's. Everyone went to bed hungry that night. I also did not realize that when a child begs for a certain food, and you make it for them, they will only take two bites before declaring they are full. The rest must go in the trash. Serving a child leftovers is the same as serving them trash, at least in the child's mind. I also did not realize that telling a child it was time for bed was an act of unmentionable cruelty, almost as bad as telling a child it was time to put the iPad away for the night.

Back then I could have written a book about all I did not know about parenting, but in my defense, until a long conversation with a foster dad named Jason during a two-hour bus ride in Kenya, I'd never thought I could be a dad. I'd never been married and had no prospects of that changing anytime soon. I did not have time for a wife, much less a family. In my work with a major child advocacy organization, I traveled abroad three to five times a month and spoke somewhere in the United States nearly every weekend that I was home. Although

I owned a nice three-bedroom house in Denver, I barely lived in it. Most of the time I rented it on a short-term basis just so that it could be occupied.

But my busy life was not the only reason I thought I'd never become a dad. My own father was not exactly the kind of role model to inspire me. He both physically and verbally abused me nearly every day. I had even witnessed my father kill a man with his bare hands after the man was caught breaking into a house. I don't think my father or the other men in the village meant to kill the thief, but once they started beating him they could not stop themselves. I believed it was only a matter of time before my father lost control while beating me and killed me. That's why I ran away at age ten. For the next five years I lived on the streets of Kampala, Uganda. My story would have ended there if not for the kindness of a stranger. A man named James rescued me from the streets and enrolled me in a boarding school. When school was out of session, I lived with James and his wife and family. Foster care was not a term used in Uganda, but that's what this was. James and his wife became my foster parents until I graduated from high school and moved off to college.

Even with James's influence, I never thought I could become a good father. For most of my adult life, I was so afraid that I might be like my father that I did not even dare dream about becoming a dad. Deep down I would have loved to have a family, but my fear of becoming my father kept me from ever pursuing it. That's part of what drove me to choose my career. I knew I could make a difference in the lives of children all over the world who were just like me. It was my way of paying forward the kindness that had been shown to me.

Eventually I got over my fears of becoming my father. However, parenthood still seemed like an impossible dream for me as a single man from Africa. Adopting internationally was out, since I was not married. I also doubted (wrongly) that I could become a foster dad in the American system as a single man. Single moms, yes. Single dads, probably not. Then, once I discovered I was allowed to foster, I assumed the cultural gap between an African man and an American child would be too wide to cross. I never witnessed a loving, caring father in my home. What did I know about how to effectively parent a child?

In spite of all of that, here I am. A dad. At the time of this writing, I have fostered forty-two children and adopted three. I currently have five children in my home and have had as many as seven at one time, and all as a single dad. Getting here took changing jobs, moving to a cheaper state to live, and trading in my Infiniti FX45 for a soccer mom van, but it was worth it.

Like every first-time parent, I had no idea what I was getting myself into when my first kid walked in the door. I thought I did, with my hours upon hours of training and reading. I had also lived the life of a child in the foster care system. I knew what it meant to live in survival mode where you cannot let your guard down to trust anyone. I knew what it was like to suffer abuse and to blame yourself for it rather than your parent. I knew how it felt to be rejected by the one who is supposed to love you, and how every good deed from a stranger always came with strings attached. Love was not normal on the streets where I grew up. Neither was kindness or even basic human decency. I believed my experiences gave me insight into the children who would come into my life.

Because I had lived a Ugandan version of the foster care life, I made up my mind to become the father I had always longed for. In other words, I thought back to what my dad had done, and I determined to do the exact opposite.

I never felt heard as a child. I would listen to my children.

Nothing I ever did for my father was good enough. He found fault in everything I did. I would do my best to speak encouragement into my children.

Growing up, my family was very poor. Most weeks we ate one meal every other day. I wished I had a father who would simply tell me, "Peter, everything is going to be all right." But my father never said anything to give me a glimpse of hope. With my foster children, one of my top goals was to always give them hope for the future.

My father could not speak to me, only yell. I would try not to raise my voice.

Everything I did was wrong in my father's eyes, which is why he beat me. Whenever my children were in the wrong, I would try to turn it into a teachable moment.

More than anything, I wanted my children to feel seen, heard, and known and to understand they had value and were important, all things I never received from my own father.

Even though deep down I knew better, I still hoped that when I expressed love to my children in this way, they would respond in kind. I envisioned children who rarely acted out, rarely threw fits, and never rejected my love. I had a fantasy of children living a happy, contented life in my home while butterflies danced around us and birds sang songs of joy.

And then my first kid walked through the door, and fantasy quickly met reality. Within the first twelve hours I questioned why I chose this life. What made me think I could actually do this? But I didn't have time to doubt myself. I had a five-year-old boy who needed me. Ready or not, I was a dad, and I had to figure this out—and fast. That was the first of many lessons I had to learn quickly when I first became a parent, along with, of course, learning how to follow the directions on the blue box of mac and cheese.

As I've interacted with other parents, I've discovered these are lessons all of us can use. Whether our children come to us through the foster care system, adoption, or childbirth, every parent struggles with feeling like they have no idea what they are doing. I do not claim that the book you hold in your hand is *the* authoritative guide you've been searching for. Instead, think of this book as a journal from a fellow traveler, one struggling parent to another.

As a single parent eight thousand miles away from any grandparents or aunts and uncles who might step in to help me out, I've had to learn the lessons in this book quickly. The first section is "Lessons I Wish I'd Known Before I Became a Dad." Believe me, no matter how prepared you think you are, all of your preconceived ideas of how to raise a child will shatter as fast as my first placement shattered a window in my home. I want to warn you ahead of time of some of the challenges that lie ahead so that when you face them, you will know you are not alone.

The second section is "Lessons That Guide My Parenting Style." I learned all the wrong things to do from my own father. More than all the rest, these are the lessons where I took everything my father did and chose to do the opposite. His mistakes did not doom me, and neither will yours doom you.

The final section, "Lessons Specifically for Foster and Adoptive Parents," may focus on the challenges foster and adoptive parents face, but these lessons can be beneficial to any parent. I know many books have been written on foster parenting, and I have read most of them. Unlike most of those authors, I am not an expert with advanced degrees but a parent just like you. I've learned these lessons as well as all the others in this book through the fire of parenthood. They have helped me as a dad to a lot of hurting children. I hope they will help you as well.

SECTION 1

LESSONS I WISH I'D KNOWN BEFORE I BECAME A DAD

2

No Matter How Prepared You Think You Are, You Will Quickly Reach a Point Where You Question Your Decision to Become a Parent

It took exactly twelve hours into my life as a dad for me to find myself in the middle of a situation I did not know how to handle. Kaine, my five-year-old first placement, had thrown his head back into a window, shattering it and raining glass down upon himself. Not that he noticed the glass or the cuts to the back of his head. He was too busy screaming because I had told him it was time for breakfast. To my great relief, the cuts to the back of Kaine's head were minor. I really didn't want to spend part of my first day as a dad in the ER explaining suspicious-looking injuries to doctors, nurses, and caseworkers.

Eventually I was able to calm Kaine down by using the tried-and-true parenting technique I'm sure even Adam and Eve used with their kids: bribery. I held up my iPad and asked, "Do you want to watch a cartoon?" It was like a switch flipped. He went from out of control to perfectly calm. Once he finished watching the cartoon he looked up at me and said, "Will you hold me now?"

The rest of the day was fairly uneventful, until I told him it was time for bed. He exploded again, crying and screaming at the top of his lungs. Three hours later, he finally got too tired to cry and again asked me to hold him. That simple request gave me my first parental insight: his fits had nothing to do with me. They came when he was comfortably doing one thing and I told him it was time for something else. With that in mind, I tried something new the next day. I let him watch another cartoon while I cooked breakfast, but this time, I told him ahead of time how long he could watch and what we were going to do when it was done. I even gave him a countdown for how much longer he had left on the iPad. My strategy worked, and not just with breakfast but throughout the day! It worked so well, and his behavior improved so much over the next day or so, that I made my next rookie mistake. I decided to reward Kaine with a special trip to that one place where a kid can be a kid: Chuck E. Cheese. Before Kaine came into my life, Chuck E. Cheese wasn't exactly high on my list of favorite pizza places. After taking Kaine, it still isn't, but that has nothing to do with the restaurant.

Having never been to Chuck E. Cheese, I did not realize how the place throws even the most chill, stable human being into sensory overload. The loud music, the flashing lights, the bells ringing nonstop as machines spit out tickets, and all the kids yelling and running around. To top it all off, a guy was walking around in a mouse suit. It was all almost more than I could take. None of this, however, seemed to faze Kaine. He took off running into the heart of the beast as soon as we walked in. I could barely keep up with him. Kaine bounced from machine to machine and ride to ride, looking at everything.

"Just tell me which one you want to play, and I'll get some tokens for you," I said. Kaine ignored me. He ran straight to the Pop-A-Shot game, squeezed in front of the boy playing on the machine, grabbed the basketball, and launched it at the basket. Everything happened so fast that the kid who lost his basketball didn't have time to react.

When Kaine tried to get the next ball, I stopped him before the other kid could do anything. "I'm sorry," I said to the kid. Then, I took Kaine by the hand to move him out of the kid's way. "Kaine, no, you can't do that. You can't just grab the ball out of someone else's hands. If you want to play this game, you will have to wait your turn."

"Nooooooo!" Kaine screamed and kicked me as hard as he could. He then clamped his teeth onto my arm that was trying to move him. I yanked my hand back, which gave Kaine the opening he needed. He took off running and screaming and darting between adults and kids and games and rides. I tried to catch him, but since he was five and I was not, he could slip through gaps so quickly I had no chance of catching him. Not only was he running, he kept screaming louder and louder until everyone in the place stopped what they were doing and looked at us. I ignored them because all I could think was that at any moment Kaine was going to head straight out the doors and run through the parking lot and into the street. Having a child run over in front of Chuck E. Cheese wasn't exactly how I imagined my first weekend as a dad.

Finally, I got close enough to Kaine to lunge and catch hold of his shirt. I reeled him in, picked him up kicking and scream-ing, and started for my car. Holding on to him was nearly impossible. His legs and arms flailed around while he kept trying to bite my arm. Every eye was on us, but by this point, I didn't care what people thought of me. All I wanted to do was get him to my car, put him in the back seat, and let him kick and scream until he wore himself out.

Just as I reached my vehicle, a car rolled slowly past us, windows down. The woman in the driver's seat stared a hole through me while talking on her phone. I knew exactly what she was thinking and who she was calling. Here was a Black man with a screaming and squirming child that clearly looked nothing like him. Everything about the situation screamed child abduction.

Great. That's all I need.

The woman drove off, but I heard sirens in the distance. They kept getting louder. Meanwhile, Kaine kept kicking and screaming inside my car.

I didn't have a lot of time, but I knew driving away would be a huge mistake. I also thought that if the police rolled up and saw a screaming child in the back seat, at best I'd end up on the ground in handcuffs. Nothing in foster care training told me how to get out of this one, so I again resorted to bribery. "Kaine, if you will stop screaming, I'll let you watch a cartoon on my phone."

Kaine immediately stopped screaming and said, "Okay."

"Let's do that outside of the car, buddy," I replied.

I figured if the police rolled up and saw Kaine calm and happy, there was less of a chance they might think I was kidnapping him. A few minutes later, a police car pulled into the parking lot and two officers got out. I smiled as I explained the situation. Neither one cracked a smile back. Both kept looking at me suspiciously. I gave them my driver's license, which I knew would clear everything up. Every foster parent in Oklahoma is on file with all the police departments for moments like this. A few moments later one of the officers came back and said something like, "Thank you, Mr. Mutabazi," and they left. Never in my life have I been so happy to have my name on a police list!

When I finally got home and got Kaine to bed for the night, I could not help but think, *I quit a career and turned my entire life upside down FOR THIS?! What have I gotten myself into?*

Then another thought slipped in.

Maybe I should call the social worker and have them place Kaine somewhere else and go back to my old life.

As soon as that thought flashed in my head, I felt guilty. *What kind of parent thinks things like this?*

All in This Together

Here's the secret I soon learned: all parents think things like this! Every parent I've talked to, whether they became a parent through biology or the foster care system, has had a moment when they questioned their decision to have kids. And by that I mean *seriously* questioned, as in thinking they had been crazy to get themselves into this mess. My moment came when I made the mistake of taking a five-year-old to a place designed to throw him immediately into sensory overload. For my collaborator, Mark, his moment came the first night after bringing his first newborn baby home from the hospital. Around midnight his daughter started crying, and nothing he and his wife did could make her stop. As he rocked his screaming child, all he could think was, *Why did we think we could do this?*

Here's the good news. When you have these thoughts, not only does it mean you are normal but it also means you have taken a very important step in your journey as a parent. Every new parent has lots of ideas and expectations about what parenthood will be like. We have these little fantasies about how our children will act and how they will respond to our love and who they will be when they grow up. The faster these fantasies get blown up—with the police called to a Chuck E. Cheese or whatever your moment is—the better. If we cling to expectations that are detached from reality, we will always find ourselves overwhelmed by unexpected outbursts or strange behavior. To effectively parent any child, we need to lose our fantasies and become a real parent in the real world.

This does not mean these moments become any less difficult. For every day of the first few weeks I had Kaine, I wondered when the phone would ring with another call from the school telling me to come down because he had turned over a table or hit another child or had some other wild outburst. And these calls did come often, although their frequency greatly decreased the longer he was with me.

I soon learned that when I find myself in difficult parenting situations (and unfortunately, they always keep coming), it's best for me to step back, take a deep breath, and realize that I can figure out a solution. It may take me several attempts to discover what will work for that particular child, but eventually, I will find something. I know that to be true because a child in distress does not want to stay in distress. They do not like losing control any more than we like dealing with them when they've lost control. When I can step back and quiet the panic inside of me, I will see a way forward. What works today may not work tomorrow, even with the same child! (That's another secret of parenting no one ever tells you going in.) But I know that if I keep control of myself, I can find a solution.

For Foster and Adoptive Parents

When a child first comes into your home, they will most likely be on their best behavior. The reason is simple: they believe they will go back to their parents in a few days. Then a week passes. And another week. And another week. And then their anger and trauma come spilling out—all of it aimed at you! What did you do to deserve this? You showed this child love. In the child's mind, they now realize that accepting your love means giving up on Mom and Dad, which they refuse to do. That's why their anger explodes on you. When it happens, you will most likely wonder two things: (1) *What happened to the beautiful, loving, well-behaved child I had yesterday?* (2) *Why did I get myself into this?* When this finally happens, go back to the beginning of this chapter. I wrote it for you.

3

You Cannot Expect a Child to Learn and Grow if You Do Not Learn and Grow as a Parent

I first noticed the smell. From the age of ten until I turned fifteen, I lived next to a garbage dump. I know the smell of rotting food. I hate that smell. When I lived on the street, my friends and I used to soak rags in diesel and put them over our noses. Most did it to get a little high, but I did it more to escape the smell. And now the smell had invaded my house.

Then I saw the ants. Lots and lots of ants. Every month I paid an exterminator to keep bugs out of my house, but now someone had invited the ants right back in. I had a pretty good idea who the culprit was and why he did it. Joseph had not lived with me long, but long enough for me to learn he hoarded food. He was one my first hoarders, but he wouldn't be my last.

Food hoarding is not unusual in children who have lived with food insecurity. They come from homes where food is scarce.

Whenever they happen to have food available, their instinct is to grab as much of it as they can and hide it to keep anyone else from stealing their stash. I know this not just from observation but from experience. I did the same thing when I first moved from the streets to boarding school. I didn't believe the cafeteria people when they told me we would have three meals a day, every day. Better to stash some food away just in case than go hungry.

Even though I knew why Joseph did what he did, it did not make me any less annoyed to discover ants crawling in and out of a stinky drawer filled with bits of old food. I knew food insecurity could be a big problem for kids like him, which is why I made sure I had far more than enough food at every meal. On top of that, the pantry was filled with snacks he could grab at any time. There was absolutely no reason for him to hoard food.

And food hoarding wasn't even the worst of it.

The first time I discovered Joseph had carried part of his dinner upstairs to his room and hidden it in a drawer, I asked him about it. He denied knowing anything.

"I didn't do it," he lied to my face.

I don't have a lot of rules in my house, but not lying to me is at the top of the list. Even more, the act of taking food felt like he was stealing from me. If he had asked, I would have gladly made him more food and served it to him in our dining room. But instead of asking, he took without permission. That's the definition of stealing. Again, I don't have a lot of rules, but not stealing from me is also near the top of the list. On top of everything else, his socking food away in his sock drawer felt like he was punishing me. I was trying to give him everything he needed and to provide a nice life for him. In return he made my house stink and filled it with ants. What was I going to do with this kid?!

I faced a dilemma. Joseph was engaging in behavior that could not continue. It had to stop right away, or the ants were going to claim my house as their own. Joseph had also broken two major rules in the Mutabazi household. I hated to think what my father would have done to me in this situation. He beat me all the time without me doing anything wrong. I would never do to a child what my father did to me, but surely there had to be some form of correction I could use, perhaps taking away some privileges until Joseph learned to stop hiding his dinner in his room. After all, that's what all parents do, right?

As it turns out, "what all parents do" is rarely what needs to be done. All of us come into parenting with preconceived ideas of how to deal with our children in whatever situation we find ourselves. None of us like to think of this as putting ourselves in a box, but that's exactly what we do. Especially if our rules and our responses to our children do not grow and develop as we learn more as a parent.

This was true for me and Joseph.

Rather than punish Joseph, I sat down with him and asked him a simple question. "How did this food get in your room?"

He looked me in the eye with all sincerity and said, "I think the food walked in here."

There it was, another lie. On top of that, it was a ridiculous lie. I could have yelled something like, "How stupid do you think I am?! Food doesn't walk around the house. You carried that food in here, and you will stop doing that *immediately*!"

I could have, but I didn't.

Instead, I took a deep breath and replied, "Okay. Please, next time you see food walking up the stairs, will you tell me so that I can stop it?"

Joseph smiled at me and said, "Okay. I'll do that."

A few days later I found more food in his room. Again, I did not yell. Instead I said, "Joseph, you said you were going to tell me the next time you saw food walking in here, but you didn't."

"Okay. I'm sorry. Next time I will tell you," Joseph said.

We played this game for several days until the food stopped walking up the stairs. At the same time, I made a second snack basket like the one I already kept on the counter in the kitchen. I placed this one at the top of the stairs near Joseph's room. Now food was accessible to him anytime he wanted it. And, bonus for me, all the snacks were prepackaged so they didn't stink or attract ants.

Think Outside the Box

I wish I could say that I came up with this strategy right after I first discovered the hoarded food. It actually took me several months to get there. To find that solution, I first had to think outside the box. My goal was not just to get a child to stop hiding food in his room. No, my primary goal was to help my child overcome his food insecurity and realize he was now in a safe place. It took me a solid year of eating three meals every day at the boarding school before I finally stopped hiding food. I knew what it was like to be in Joseph's shoes, but I had no idea how to help him work through what he was feeling. I thought simply providing meals and having snacks available at all times would be enough. But hoarding food is part of the survival instinct. So, to solve the issue, I had to dismantle my preconceived ideas about what the practical solution should be before I could truly learn how to help my child.

The same principle holds true for every child. One of our goals as parents is to teach and train our children as we prepare them to survive in a bigger world. However, only those willing to learn can effectively teach. The question is how to "learn" as a parent while living in the midst of the parenting chaos.

First, we must be willing to learn. I grew up in a house where it was understood that my father was always right . . . even when he was wrong. My father was an extreme case, but many of us as parents carry the same attitude, even if we grew up in healthy families. Our parents were always right, and the way they did things was the way things needed to be done. But what if the way your parents always did things for you does not work for your children? We must be willing to turn loose of our preconceived ideas as we learn from our children and grow as parents.

Second, I find it valuable after every confrontation or unusual episode with my kids to take time to review my actions to see what I can do better the next time. (And there will always be a next time.) I ask myself if I reacted or responded to my child. Did I focus on teaching, or did I go straight to trying to change behavior that was driving me crazy? Did I get on my child's level and communicate in a way they could understand? Was my correction effective in helping my child overcome, even if temporarily, whatever they were dealing with? I can stay calm and communicate effectively, but if I deliver the wrong message, I haven't done my kids any favors. Every crisis, every situation that leaves me thinking, *Wait, what?!*, is a chance for me to learn, but only if I set aside time to do that.

Finally, much of what I have learned as a parent has come from other parents who face the same daily challenges I do. Find a group of parents who are in the same stage of parenting and learn together. Sometimes I find that none of us have any answers for what we are going through. Those are some of the best times with a group because the biggest thing I learn is that I am not alone. Just knowing this gives me hope.

For Foster and Adoptive Parents with Biological Children

One of the out-of-the-box revelations parents with both biological and foster/adoptive children have shared with me is the insight that the approaches used with their bio children will not work with fosters. The way we speak to them, the rules we have for them, the way in which we discipline—everything is different for a child who comes into your home after being pulled out of theirs. Your bio child instinctively trusts you from birth, while a foster child instinctively distrusts you from the moment they walk in the door. A raised voice of disappointment with a bio child is often the only form of punishment needed. As children, we want to please our parents. A raised voice to a child who came out of a dysfunctional home has the opposite effect. Many of the children who have come into my home want to push me to the point of anger. When I raise my voice, I'm signaling that they are winning. Remaining calm throws them off their game. They don't know what to do when an authority figure stays in control of themselves and doesn't lash out with anger. In the same way, in a healthy home, a hug is a sign of love and security. It is normal. For a child who has been abused, a hug is a warning sign that you want something from them. When they see you approach with your arms open, their fight-or-flight instinct kicks in.

But that's not normal, you may be thinking. Exactly! You cannot always take a "normal" parental approach. What works for a child in one set of circumstances will not work with another. In the same way, what worked with a child at age five will not work when they are fifteen. As parents, we are continually learning, growing, and adjusting our parenting style to meet our children where they are, as they are. But we cannot expect them to learn and grow if we are not willing to do the same alongside them.

4

Love Does Not Conquer All

It seems so simple. The most basic human need is love. Everybody wants to be loved. Everybody needs to be loved. Therefore, the number one thing we must do as parents is love our children. If we do that, everything else will take care of itself . . . won't it?

Many of us go into parenting believing that love will conquer all, but, in my experience, it does not. At least not at first, and sometimes not for years. It especially won't work if we only use the easy ways of expressing love to our kids, like giving hugs, making favorite meals, and buying that special toy they've wanted for a long time. Unfortunately, that kind of love only works in the movies. In real life, love is hard—painful, even. I know this all too well because I've been on both sides of the equation.

When I lived on the streets, I did not trust anyone. I could not. The moment you trusted someone, you opened yourself up to harm. I saw it every day. Most adults looked at my friends and me like we were basically human garbage. Since garbage littered the streets, we were only noticed when we annoyed someone. That happened a lot since we had to beg, steal, or do whatever else it took to survive. We spent most of our time around a huge, open-air market next to a bus station. The shopkeepers didn't want a bunch of lost boys coming around and stealing their stuff. From time to time one of them caught one of us and beat him, but we had ways to get revenge. We discovered that when it came to vegetable stands, most people wouldn't buy anything if they saw human feces on top of the tomatoes. If the shop owner didn't want that to happen, then they wouldn't make a big deal out of it when a few plantains turned up missing. However, our tactics didn't always work. I once saw someone stuffed into several old car tires and set on fire for stealing. We all knew that was one of the risks, which is why we took steps to protect ourselves.

Angry shopkeepers were easy to understand. They had their guard up against us, and we had ours up against them. The real danger came when someone did something we never expected: they were nice to us. When you live in survival mode, every person is a potential threat. You never let anyone get close to you. However, when someone shows you kindness, something inside instinctively wants to believe it is real. Even though there are always strings attached, you want to think someone actually cares about you. So eventually, you let your guard down.

I did that with one of the female shop owners in the market. I had been on the streets a few years and no longer looked like that little ten-year-old boy who ran away from home. One day she asked me if I was hungry, and when I told her I was, she gave me a piece of fruit and a smile. I thanked her and went on my way. Over the next several days, she gave me more to eat. I started to think that perhaps there were genuinely kind people in the world. Those thoughts blew apart when this same woman demanded sexual favors in exchange for the food she had given me. I came away humiliated and angry and determined to never trust anyone again.

That is how you survive on the streets. You cannot trust anyone. You are suspicious of everyone. Every person you meet wants something from you, and every act of kindness is bait in a trap.

It was no wonder, then, that when a man named James extended genuine kindness and compassion to me, I did not believe him. I went along with him only to get close enough to steal some food from him. Yet he gave me food before I could steal it. As time went by, and the two of us got to know one another, I remained suspicious. Even when he took me off the streets and put me in a boarding school where I had a place to sleep and three meals a day, along with an education, I kept waiting for the other shoe to drop. It took years for me to learn to trust James and his family and to actually believe he loved me and would not demand anything from me in return.

Now, as a parent, I find myself on the other side of the equation. One of my foster placements was a set of three sisters. From their first day, the three of them seemed happy to be around me, which was a change from most kids in the early days of foster care. They seemed so open that I thought I could shower these girls with love and help them heal from the effects of the trauma that had landed them in foster care. When we watched television, all three wanted to sit on the sofa next to me. When they told me one of their favorite meals, I'd agree to cook it for them that very night. When I took them shopping and they'd ask to buy something with a big smile, I always said yes. Loving these girls was easy, and I just knew it would make a big difference.

That is, until I quickly came to realize this set of sisters was playing me. Yes, they'd jump down next to me on the sofa to watch their favorite show on television, but two or three minutes later, the three of them would look at one another and just move to the other side of the room. When I put a plate of their favorite food in front of them, one after another they'd slip off their chairs and not eat a bite. Or, if I left the room for a moment, I'd come back and find the dish I'd worked so hard to make in the trash. The day after our shopping trip, I went to dump something in the trash and found everything I'd bought them in the trash can. For a guy who grew up never knowing where my next meal was going to come from, never having a parent to spend time with me, and never having anyone buy me the things I wanted, these acts were more than annoying. They felt like acts of war against me personally!

However, with time I came to understand that their tactics were rooted in a different form of survival skills. When they moved across the room from me, it wasn't because all three wanted to do that; only one of them did. Whatever one sister did, they all did. If one decided to throw a gift I bought her in the trash, they all did. When one decided she didn't like her sister's favorite dish, they all refused to eat it and threw it out. It was their way of protecting one another. I wanted to tell them that they did not have to be protected from me. I wanted to tell them that I really and truly did want them to feel loved. In fact, all I wanted to do was provide a safe place for them to live and for them to feel love and acceptance for perhaps the first time in their lives. My intentions may have been right, but these girls were no more ready to drop their guards than I had been with James. No matter how unconditional my love may have been, it wasn't enough to get them to trust me.

Unconditional Love

So, what can we do as parents?

We must always remember that for love to be unconditional, it must be put to the test. And no one knows how to test your love like a child. Children are a lot like roses. They are beautiful, yes, but they still come with thorns. To love a child is to be willing to be stuck by the thorns without complaint. Love can and does make a difference, but is it not lovey-dovey hugs and good-night kisses and "Let's go to Disney World and live in the happiest place on earth." Real love is patient when patience is difficult. Real love is kind when a child is lashing out. Real love does not become angry even while being bombarded with f-bombs or, worse, enduring the silent treatment. Real love is hard. It forces us to step outside of ourselves and see the world from another perspective. But if we're willing to do that, we'll be stepping closer and closer to the kind of love our children desperately need.

We have to learn how our children understand and receive love. Otherwise it is like we are speaking English to an audience who only understands Mandarin. This goes beyond the concept of "love languages" that became popular thirty years ago. Instead, it means understanding each child for who they are. For a child like myself, who has never known what love is, a simple act of kindness can seem like a threat. For children like the three sisters in my home, protection is more important than love. Rather than be offended or hurt by the perspectives and realities our children come with, we need to understand them and remain consistent in loving them the way they need, even when it feels like our efforts are not making a difference.

For Foster and Adoptive Parents

As foster parents, we need to realize that if love is to conquer anything, it must first conquer us. I think every human being struggles to love someone when they are at their worst. With a child who has lived through trauma, it can be incredibly frustrating to keep giving and giving and giving and have the child continually lash out at us in response.

I have to be honest. When this happens, part of me wants to say, "Fine! If you don't want me as your dad, I won't be. You are on your own." That feels natural. What doesn't feel natural is to reject rejection and choose to keep on loving. Yet that's exactly what our children need.

With children who have never experienced love, the more we love them, the angrier they become and the more they push back against us. Love doesn't conquer; it triggers. It pushes a child into a vulnerable place, and the only way they know to react is to fight back.

That's what I did. The more James and his family loved me, the more it scared me. The very idea of accepting their love felt like losing what I had always fought to hold on to. Up until that point, my life had been about fighting to survive and putting up walls to protect myself before anyone could harm me. I had to do that because everywhere I looked, danger lurked. Love was not normal in my world, and we are all afraid of what is not normal.

Thankfully, my foster family did not give up on me. Love did not conquer me. Instead, it built a bridge that eventually I was ready to cross. If that's what love did for me, how can I do anything less for my children?

5

Parenting Will Expose Your Scars

I had all of my kids in the car one day. Maybe *car* is not the right word. I have a vehicle that is so big, driving it is more like piloting an ocean liner. I am not exactly a tall man, which means I have a little trouble seeing over the hood that is nearly as long as a football field. If it sounds like I am making excuses, I am! This car is not easy to navigate. That is why, when I went to park one day with the car filled up with all of my children, I ran up and over the curb. My teenage son, who was sitting in the front seat, laughed and said, "Gee, Dad, why'd they ever give *you* a driver's license?"

I tried to smile as my other kids laughed along, but it was like I'd been dragged into a time machine. Instead of being in my ocean liner–sized vehicle, I was back in my home village in Uganda with my father standing over me in anger, yelling at the top of his lungs.

"What did you do with my socks?! You can't do anything right! Do you know that?! You're worthless!"

"Dad," my son said to me, snapping me out of my trance. "Are you okay?"

"Sure," I said as I tried to think of something else to say. My kids and I joke around like this all the time. Normally I would come back with something funny, but I was having trouble thinking of anything humorous with my dad's words echoing in my head. I had to fight the urge to snap at my son and hurt him with my words like he had hurt me. I kept reminding myself that my son was not my father. My son was not trying to tear me down. He was just making a joke . . . and telling the truth! I do run over curbs from time to time.

Finally, I managed to pull myself together and said something that made my kids all laugh. Internally, however, all I could think about was how my son's words had opened a wound inside of me that I thought had long since scarred over. *Did that really just happen?* I wondered. *Does my father still have that strong of a hold on me?* Since the day I ran away from home, I had worked hard to leave all my father's verbal and physical abuse in the past. As long as I let those memories hold me down, my father was winning, and I was determined not to let that happen. I had traveled back to my home village several times and showed my father the man I had become despite him. "You did not and will not ever defeat me," I'd said through my achievements that I rubbed in his face. Up to that point, I thought I had successfully shut him out of my mind and my life. I now had to admit to myself that wasn't, in fact, the case. The scars were still there, and they still hurt.

More Scars

The ways in which my children treat food expose another huge scar from my childhood. Food was scarce for my family. My father spent most of our money on himself and left my mother to try to figure out how to provide for us kids. Going to bed hungry was a way of life. When I ran away, living on the streets was even worse. My friends and I survived on whatever we could beg or salvage from the trash or steal. When you get hungry enough, you will do literally anything for food and eat anything that is even marginally edible. I watched friends die of malnutrition or from eating something they should not have. These memories have never left me.

I left the streets at age fifteen, but I carry the scars of that time with me. Things like fear of food insecurity don't magically go away. Even today, I do not take food for granted. In my adult life, I have always done my best never to let any go to waste.

Then I had kids.

The sun comes up in the east, and kids waste food. You can count on both every single day. They waste food when the cereal they loved yesterday is the cereal they hate today. They waste food when they take two bites out of a meal you prepared just for them and declare they are full. They waste food when they take a bite out of an apple, then decide they don't want it. With kids who also came from homes where food was scarce, they waste food by piling as much as they can on their plates—more food than a three-hundred-pound football player could eat—and then throwing three-quarters of it away. And in all of this waste, they're not just exposing my scars; they're smashing them with a hammer.

Early on in my adventures of parenthood, when my child went to throw food away, I'd stop them. "What are you doing? That's good food."

"But I'm full," my child always said.

"Here, give it to me. I'll finish it off."

Yes, I tried to make sure no food was wasted by eating every leftover. It did not take long to discover that the food I did not want to go to waste went right to my waist. Eating everyone's leftovers was not an option. Still, my frustration kept building.

Every breakfast.

Every lunch.

Every dinner.

It was the same thing.

More food went in the trash than into my kids. I thought about lecturing them. I thought about telling them how I had gone to bed hungry every night and how there were still kids who went to bed hungry all over the world.

"How can you waste food when there are starving children in Sudan?" I could say.

But what good would it do? It's not like my daughter could put half of her peanut butter sandwich in a box and mail it to some starving kid somewhere. My words would only make my children feel guilty for something beyond their control.

We All Carry Scars

All of us carry scars from our pasts. Sure, mine may be different from yours, but we all have them. Even those we think we have dealt with have a way of resurfacing in our interactions with our children. I have talked through my painful memories with counselors, and they have given me great tools to help me get past them. But that doesn't mean they ever completely go away. When that happens to us as parents, what are we to do?

I believe there are two things we absolutely cannot do. First, we cannot take our anger out on our children over what someone else did in the past. Foster parents know all too well that we receive enough of that from our kids. They often lash out at us because they are angry with the bio mom who did not show up for their visitation time for the third time in a row. We know how it feels to be on the receiving end of that misplaced anger, which is why we cannot turn this around on our kids. Yes, we all have scars. When they surface through something our children do or say, we must remind ourselves that they are not the ones we are really angry with. Even when our children do something intentionally to try to trigger us, they are not the enemy. Our painful memories do not have to become their painful memories because we reacted rather than responded.

Second, we must also avoid overcompensating to try to fill the void left by our own pain. Trust me, it is easy to fall into this trap. For parents who grew up poor, we often go to the other extreme with our children and give them everything they could ever desire. Or if you're a parent who, like me, grew up with a cruel and abusive parent who used the word *punishment* to justify a beating, we can easily do just the opposite and never correct our children's behavior. In either case, we are not doing our children any favors. We do not get any sort of revenge on those who hurt us by building bubbles around our children where they will never experience any pain, any want, or any consequences from their actions.

Our primary responsibility as parents is not to ease our own pain but to help our children grow up to become responsible, independent adults. We cannot prevent our children from ever being hurt by life and never developing their own scars, nor should we try. My scars are still painful, but they helped make me into the man I am today.

Instead of choosing these unhealthy, unhelpful responses when our scars surface, we need to acknowledge them for what they are. For example, I know I am sensitive to criticism because of my past. Therefore, when my son makes a joke about my driving or my daughter takes one taste of her dinner, sticks out her tongue, and groans, "Yuck," I do not take their words as a personal attack. Instead, I pause, take a deep breath (parents need to take lots of deep breaths, it seems), and gather myself before I respond.

We need to find healthy ways to address our children's behaviors that trigger these emotions. In the case of wasted food, I have conversations with my children—conversations, not lectures. I have shared parts of my story with my children, telling them how I lived with constant hunger. Rather than try to make them feel guilty, I work to reach an agreement with them at mealtimes to start off with smaller portions.

"You can have seconds and thirds and even fourths if you are still hungry. But only take as much as you think you can eat so that less food goes in the trash," I tell them.

And because it's rooted in a healthy response rather than a reaction from a scar provoked, it works.

For Foster and Adoptive Parents (and Really for All of Us)

Every member of my family carries painful memories. At the time of this writing, I have a toddler who has been with me since before she could walk. Just because she is a baby does not mean her trauma of being removed from her bio parents at such a young age does not affect her.

All of this means that, for those of us who are foster and adoptive parents, not only will our scars be exposed but so will our children's. There are times when a child will react to a situation in a way that is so abrupt, so uncalled for, and so out of character for the child that we feel like we were just blindsided by a truck.

Where did this come from, and how can I fix it?

I find that these reactions are often the result of a wound from the past rising up in the child. They always happen at the most inopportune moments, like in the middle of church. I cannot tell you how many times one of my kids has melted down in church because they suddenly feel hungry, which triggers all their emotional responses to their history of never having enough food. Rather than become angry or frustrated, I need to be prepared. I don't worry about being embarrassed by a child's behavior. Instead, I deal with the situation at hand with the goal of working toward their healing.

Believe me, when you both carry around scars—especially the same scars—the triggering can flash back and forth like a gunfight in an old western movie. Don't let it throw you off your game. After all, sometimes our shared scars can be the greatest bridge we will ever have to bond with our children.

6

Every Belief and Conviction Will Be Tested and Every Bias Revealed

One of my foster sons and I were talking one day when I asked him a question every kid gets asked a million times: "What do you want to be when you grow up?" I expected to hear one of the usual answers.

I want to be a doctor.

I want to be a race car driver.

I want to be a firefighter.

And of course there's the one every kid today gives: *I want to be an influencer.*

If he had given me any of these responses or one of the thousands like them, I would not have been surprised. But that's not what he said. Instead my child looked at me with all sincerity and said, "I want to be a girl." I've had lots and lots of children come into my home over my time as a foster dad, and I've had some form of this conversation with nearly all of them. But this was the first time any ever said anything like this.

I should have expected his answer. When I took him to the store to buy a toy, he went straight to the Barbies and cried until I bought one for him. When he picked out his own clothes to wear to school or church, he always picked pinks and pastels rather than a superhero T-shirt. Most days, he played with his sisters rather than the other boys in the house. Unlike other sons I've raised, he was not interested in sports or action movies. When I signed one of his sisters up for ballet, he got mad at me because I didn't sign him up too. I explained that I did this so that his sister would have something all her own, but that did not make him any less angry. He was so mad that he complained to his friends at school.

"My dad is so mean that he won't let me take ballet like my sister," he told them.

I don't know what they said back, but when he came home, he said, "Hey, Dad, from now on I want to be a cowboy."

Cowboy or not, whenever my son was home with no male friends around, he continued playing with Barbies. It's just who he was. Growing up in Africa, I never heard of a boy wanting to be a girl. Today, in America at least, a lot of people still don't want to hear about it. Gender identity has become a hot political topic. States have passed laws that basically say they want all gender questions to go away. Politicians rail against gender issues and pronouns as if a boy who says he wants to be a girl will cause the death of America. On the other hand, some will find fault with me for not going to the school and confronting all those kids who made my son come home dejected and telling me he now wanted to be a cowboy when clearly he did not. But would doing that make the school environment easier for my son? Of course not. It would only make matters worse and worse until he'd never want to go back there. Or worse.

Love Is the Motivation

My point is simply this: lots of people seem to have convictions about what they would do if they were in my position. My son's situation is like any other part of parenting. Everyone believes they know exactly how to handle any and every situation—until they actually go through it themselves with their own kids. People who have never had a two-year-old may say they would never let their child throw a fit in public or defiantly tell them no more than once. All I can say is I have a toddler for the very first time as I'm writing this. You don't "let" toddlers do anything. They're going to do what they are going to do, and woe to anyone who gets in their way. In the same way, lots of people on the news and social media express their deep beliefs about children like my son and what should be done when a boy says he wants to be a girl. Of course, these are people who have never gone through this with their own children. If they ever do, I wonder what will happen to all their convictions.

Having every belief and conviction we hold put to the test is a normal part of parenting. Everything from big questions like who God is and what gender identity means to little things like how to load the dishwasher or tie your shoes can and will be flipped upside down and sideways by your kids until you don't know which way is up. This is especially true for foster and adoptive parents. You have children who were not born into your household. They may well have been in many foster homes before they came to you. You know practically nothing about them when they arrive. Your social worker can't help because they don't know that much either, beyond what caused the children to be placed in the system. In other words, these children are not going to be anything like kids who are born into your household and have lived with you their entire lives. In all likelihood, they aren't going to be like you, either.

Those of us who foster or adopt children outside of our own cultural identities experience this twice over. I am African. Most of the kids I have fostered have been White. I am Ugandan. All but two of my forty-plus children were born in America. I grew up in a culture where children never, ever misbehaved in front of strangers. When we went to church, or school, or even out in our village around other adults, we were always on our absolute best behavior. That is not a typical American view.

Still, you do not have to come from a completely different culture from your children to have your convictions and beliefs challenged by them. No matter how hard you try, and no matter how sternly you teach your beliefs to your children, they are going to make up their own minds. All we can really do is model the best example we can so that our lives match our words. In the long run, we have very little control over what our children will do with what we teach them. Some will embrace our example, and some will reject everything we ever do or say, but all children will have questions. Our job is to create a safe environment where they feel the freedom to have real, honest conversations about anything and everything, no matter how uncomfortable the topics may make us.

I know many parents will disagree with me. There are those out there who believe I should have done everything I could to reinforce my son's masculinity and squash his ideas about being a girl. He said he wanted to be a cowboy, so I should have taken him to the stables to learn how to ride a horse. The two of us should've sat down and watched every cowboy movie ever made. Instead of letting him get to know Barbie, I needed to introduce him to John Wayne. But buying my son a cowboy hat and teaching him to rope and ride could never solve my son's "problem" because, to him, there was no problem.

When he pulled a Barbie doll off the shelf, he was expressing who he was. Because I chose to parent my son for who he was rather than who I wanted him to be, I bought him the doll he wanted and not the superhero action figures boys were "supposed" to play with. Will he still want to be a girl when he is in his teens, twenties, and beyond? I have no way of knowing. What I do know is that I cannot let my own convictions and biases change the way I love my children. After all, unconditional love means *unconditional*, whatever choices our children make.

And This Is Where It Gets Messy

Our convictions and beliefs will be pushed to the limit, but that does not mean we need to abandon them when our children do not share them. Loving our children does not mean we have to endorse every life choice they make. Unconditional love means we remain constant in our love for them while also giving them the freedom to do what they will.

For example, I am a Christian. I love Jesus. When I look back at my life, I see God's hand at work. As a dad, I could not do what I do without God. Part of the way I live out my Christian life is by taking my children to church. I want them to know God loves them unconditionally. However, my beliefs about God often do not match my children's experiences. When I tell them God loves them, it usually leads to a lot of questions.

If God loves me, why did he take my parents away?

If God loves me, why did he let my mom's boyfriend abuse me?

If God loves me and he can do anything, why did my parents not come back?

I've had my kids come home from Sunday school and tell me that the teacher told them that if they prayed hard enough and believed with all their heart, God would answer their prayers. "I'm praying I get to go back to my mom," my child will announce. I will never doubt God, but when this parent the child is praying for has already had all their parental rights terminated, I know my child is never going back to them. Nor should they. Again, I know God can do miracles, and he can set addicts free, but if the addict doesn't want to be set free, then what? What is God to do? Even worse, how am I to ever explain this to my child in a way that will not wreck their faith in God and in me? I can't.

That is why, once my children turn fifteen, I do not force them to go to church with me. Whether they go or not is completely their decision, as is the decision of what they will do with Jesus. Believe or not, follow or reject, the choice is theirs to make. I cannot make it for them; no one can. Whatever they decide does not change the way I love my kids, nor does it change the way I treat them day to day. The same is true for any other decisions they make that may be the opposite of what I would choose for them. They make their own choices and live with the consequences, good and bad. My job is to be their dad—to be there for them whatever they decide to do.

That is my point of view. Here's what our kids often see: if we do not affirm and enthusiastically endorse all their life decisions, they think that means we do not love them. When they make bad decisions and we do not shield them from the consequences or rescue them when everything blows up in their faces, they think that means we do not love them. If the beliefs and convictions that guide how we parent seem too rigid, children see only rules, and rules mean we do not trust them. Therefore, they think we do not love them.

In other words, moms and dads, it feels like we cannot win. There will be days when whatever we do is wrong and everything is our fault, and at some point we realize the biggest belief we have that will be pushed to the limit is our belief that having kids was a good idea! Some days it feels like no matter what we do we are going to screw up our kids and leave them paying high therapist's bills for their entire adult lives. But hopefully by then our kids will have kids, and we will get to enjoy the wonders of being grandparents while our kids worry about screwing up their kids' lives! Because, of course, by then everything will be their fault (at least in their kids' eyes), but we will be the beloved grandparents who are everything the parents are not. Maybe that's the reason we all have children in the first place!

Thankfully, we also get to see the fruit of our consistency. Nothing brings greater joy than to see our kids grow to a place where they begin to get it, and they finally value and understand what we were trying to teach them all along. This is the long view that we must always keep in front of us. In the middle of one of those horrible days when we get to hear our children (most likely teenagers) list all the ways we keep ruining their lives, it's easy to give up. But those days do not last. Part of the purpose in being tested is that we come out on the other side stronger. You may not always see the fruit in your kids' lives, but you will see it in yourself. And in the end, that makes it worth it.

7

You Won't Always Like Your Kids

If someone had told me that I would not always like my kids before I became a father, I would have: (1) laughed that this was impossible, and (2) questioned that person's fitness for being a parent.

You won't always like your kids?! Inconceivable! Being a dad is the greatest experience in the world. I love my kids more than life itself. Every real parent treasures every moment of every day that we get to spend with our little angels. What could any of my children do to make me not like them?

Forty-two kids (and counting) later, I now have a list. I find it very difficult to like my kids when they . . .

Lie to my face repeatedly.

Steal from me and then lie about it when I can see the thing they've stolen is right there in their room and they are the only person who ever goes in their room and yet they still tell me they didn't take it as if I am blind or stupid or both.

Scream at me that I am the worst father in the world.

Punch holes in the walls of my house I worked very hard to make nice.

Hit me.

Threaten to hit me.

Kick me.

Bite me.

Bury me with f-bombs when I try to do something nice for them.

Completely ignore me as a way of punishing me for doing something nice for them.

Lie some more.

Steal some more.

Before I became a father, I never expected to have days when I would sit in my car in the driveway after coming home, thinking about how much I dreaded walking into my own home because I knew what was waiting for me inside. I have had children who, once I finally forced myself to go inside my house, made me wish I had not. As soon as I saw their faces my gut would tense and the hair on the back of my neck would stand on end, and I immediately went into fight-or-flight mode. They may not have done anything yet, but I knew they were basically heat-seeking missiles just looking for an excuse to get mad at me. Even worse have been the children whose primary form of entertainment was a game they could have called "Let's Torment Dad." Antagonizing me caused pure hell for me but filled them with joy. I wish I was exaggerating. It has been more than exhausting. There have been days I absolutely hated being a dad. In those moments, when I thought of my pre-parental days, I wished I could build a time machine to go back and make a different decision.

Navigating the Inconceivable and the Inevitable

Some of you may find yourself agreeing with my children who call me the worst dad in the world. What I now say to you I mean with all love and compassion: your time is coming. The specific actions your children take may be very different from mine, but unfortunately, a time is coming when they will push you to the brink. Then, just for fun, they'll give you another hard shove. This day may not come when your children are young, or even when they are teenagers. I have spoken with many parents who found themselves wrestling with these feelings for the first time after their children became adults and started treating their parents in ways that made them wonder what they had ever done to deserve this.

Whenever it comes, when you find yourself thinking, *You know, I really don't like this kid*, and you beat yourself up because you think your kids are now right and you are, in fact, the worst parent in the world, remember this: your feelings are completely normal.

Completely. Normal.

Of course, these feelings are also reciprocated. Our kids, too, will have days where they don't like us as parents very much either. Normal or not, no one wants to find themselves sitting in the driveway dreading going inside and seeing their own children.

But it happens. Not often, but it happens.

Rather than feel guilty, we need to recognize one of the primary reasons we all have days like this. Simply put, we are fallen human beings and so are our children. Fallen human beings can cause strong negative emotional reactions in each other without even trying. That's part of what happens in every relationship we have! Spouses who have been married for months or decades don't always like one another. Lifelong best friends do not always like one another. When the dogs jump over the couch and race to the door to bark at nothing eighty-seven times a day, dog owners don't always like their dogs. Even the most devout Christians, if they are honest, will admit there are times they get upset with God and don't like him very much. Having these feelings is a normal part of being human and interacting with and loving others. Why would interacting with our children and loving them be any different?

Dealing with Our Feelings in a Healthy Way

For our own sanity, rather than hide these feelings and pretend we never have strong negative reactions to our children or go to the other extreme and lash out because we are angry, the healthiest thing we can do is be honest with ourselves and acknowledge the emotions we feel. For those who have a partner in parenting, it is good to have times together away from the children when you can honestly talk about what you feel without the other judging you for it. As a single parent, I have that conversation with myself often. When I find myself sitting in my car wondering if I want to go into my house or drive away and never come back, I try to pinpoint exactly why I feel that way and what prompted these feelings. For me, looking beyond the behavior that makes me dislike my child and finding its root cause helps me process my own anger toward them when it comes up. When one of my sons showered me with f-bombs after I signed him up for driver's ed, he later admitted that he got so angry with me because he could not believe anyone would do something nice for him. This revelation did not make me enjoy his verbal barrage, but it helped the two of us work past it. In the end, our relationship was stronger for it.

Realizing I have legitimate emotional responses to my children's actions does not give me an excuse to respond negatively to them. As parents, we cannot allow our children's words and actions to be our kryptonite. We cannot allow them to throw us into an emotional tailspin and surrender control to them. I cannot tell you how absolutely tiresome it is to have children come into my home who find a great deal of pleasure in antagonizing me. If all my kids did this, I would have stopped being a foster parent a long time ago. But when it does happen, the more I let those kids get under my skin, the more fun they have. It took a few such children before I realized what they were doing. Once I did, I learned to stop reacting no matter what they do. The calmer I stay, the less fun they have—until they finally give up the game.

Most important of all, even when we don't like our kids, we must always keep in mind that loving someone unconditionally means loving them unconditionally. While I may have those rare days when I do not like my children, there is never a day when I stop loving them. Every day, even on the hardest days, I choose to love my children whether they reciprocate or not.

In 1 Corinthians 13:4–7, Paul describes love like this:

Love is patient and kind. Love is not jealous or boastful or proud or rude. It does not demand its own way. It is not irritable, and it keeps no record of being wronged. It does not rejoice about injustice but rejoices whenever the truth wins out. Love never gives up, never loses faith, is always hopeful, and endures through every circumstance.

This means that when a child screams, "I hate it here! You are not my dad! You are the worst father in the whole wide world!" I can choose to be kind and not hold their words against them. When a child steals from me and lies to my face after I find the stolen item sitting on their bed, I can choose to be patient rather than explode in anger. When a child pushes me to my limit, I can choose not to give up on them and endure through every circumstance they may put me and my family through.

This does not mean I never discipline a child. Instead, it means I don't allow my emotions to rule how I correct my children when I do so. Love is not easy, especially on the days when we feel anything but loving toward one of our children. Yet it is days like this when love is truly shown to be real.

For Foster and Adoptive Parents

Loving another person takes a lot of energy. When we love someone, we naturally expect them to love us in return. But we cannot carry this expectation into foster parenting. It will set us up for not only disappointment but resentment toward the child and the system. Then, ultimately, we'll burn out. We cannot expect a child to fill any kind of need we may have for love. They already feel rejection from their bio parents. The last thing they need from us is for us to shun them if they don't show sufficient gratitude for bringing them into our home.

Unfortunately, a lot of foster parents wrestle with exactly that. One of the things that can make it hard for us to like our children is when they do not appreciate what we are doing for them. Remember, though, we are the ones who chose to become foster parents. Our children did not ask to be thrown into this system. To them, we are often part of the system that took them away from Mom or Dad. Therefore, we cannot take their rejection of us personally.

Does this mean it hurts any less to love a child who does not love us in return? Of course not! Having an emotional reaction to our children rejecting us is normal. Acknowledge the hurt.

Name the emotion. I also recommend seeking counseling and other support. As caregivers, we can only provide the quality of support that we ourselves are open to receiving. Therefore, don't be afraid to ask for help or to open up to others who are safe for you. Our kids need that from us, even when they make it very, very difficult for us to like them.

Don't worry, those days will pass . . . probably.

8

Moms and Dads, You Can Do More Than You Ever Thought Possible

Right after I started writing this book, I received the following message from a mom:

> I have had the urge to write to you so many times. I am a mother through adoption. Today, reading your phrase on the struggle to over-come our own trauma so it doesn't get into our parenting style. . . . That's what hurts me most. I know my kids know they are loved, [and] they are grown now, but I really wish I would have been a better mother. Beyond all my self-compassion, I still feel sorry about this.

One phrase jumps off the page at me: "I really wish I would have been a better mother." I think every parent has felt this way at some point. I know I have. I wish I had been a more patient father when one of my daughters complained that she felt like she was about to throw up . . . again. She felt like she was going to throw up nearly every day. The first few times I took her to the doctor, but he could find nothing wrong. Still, she kept coming down with the same "sickness" day after day. I gave her over-the-counter medicine for her upset stomach, but it did not help. The longer this went on, the more I found myself wishing she'd just throw up all over the car and finally show she really was sick! What kind of father thinks such thoughts?

I also wish I could have been more sensitive to one of my sons who woke me up in the middle of the night, for what felt like every night, forever.

"I had a horrible nightmare," he'd cry as he walked into my room.

Like a good dad, I'd hold him and calm him and assure him that it was only a dream. Once he stopped crying, I'd take him back to his room and tuck him back in his bed. Then I'd go back to bed to try to get back to sleep—only to have him wake me up again with another bad dream. We'd go through the whole routine again and again, until I ended up sleeping on the floor in his room. Even though I grew up sleeping on the hard ground, I really, really enjoy sleeping on my own soft mattress now. Many mornings after sleeping on his floor, I'd wake up stiff and achy and not in a great mood. Those weren't my best mornings as a dad.

I'm also not proud of the day when one of my kids who had aged out of the foster care system and went off in search of their birth parents wanted to move back into my house. I told them no. I had good reasons. At that point, I really felt like the only way to get through to them was to exercise some tough love, but I still felt horrible about it. It wasn't just tough love. As a parent of older kids, sometimes I feel like my kids ignore me and make decisions that are basically throwing themselves off a cliff. I know it is a cliff, and I warn them and tell them to consider a different way. They're like, *What do you know?*

I am going to do what I want! Then they go flying off the cliff and crash, with no one to go down to the bottom to put them back together except me. I get tired of putting my kids back together. So I say, "No, you can't move back into my house right now." I tell them if they really want to come back, they must do this and this and this first. In other words, all the things I told them to do instead of jumping off that cliff. I know what I am telling them is for their own good, but I still feel like a bad dad when I do it.

I can't help but wonder why feeling like a terrible parent comes so naturally to most of us. I'd argue this is especially true for moms. All we can see are our "failures" as parents, and we end up beating ourselves up over them. Even worse, we let our feelings drive our parenting style, and we end up making decisions for our kids out of guilt. Let me tell you, parental guilt to a child is like blood in the water to a shark. They can smell it, and they will take advantage of it.

Failure Is Not an Option

Instead of focusing on all our failures, here's a lesson I have learned through being a dad: as parents, we can do more than we ever thought possible. Most of you moms and dads out there, you're amazing. Every single day, you're doing more than you might even realize and certainly more than you thought possible before parenthood.

Before I became a dad, I did not know that I could have a child tell me she was sick over and over again and, instead of losing all my patience, be able to see the pattern of when and why she complained that she was about to throw up. It came to me when the school called me (again!) to tell me my daughter was not feeling well. When I got to the school, I discovered my daughter had not told her new third-grade teacher that she was about to puke. Instead she went to the second-grade teacher she adored and told her. A light bulb came on. This was my daughter's way of getting people she loved to spend time with her. She had figured out that people pay far more attention to a sick child. When she needed attention, suddenly she felt like she was going to throw up her breakfast. And it worked nearly every time. Not only was I able to figure out this pattern that had nearly driven me crazy, but I was also able to work with her to find healthy ways for her to spend quality time with people who meant a lot to her.

Before I became a dad, I didn't know I could do anything like that.

I was also able to figure out that my son's nightmares were really a way for him to be near me. He was not faking the nightmares; they were real. However, I also discovered he'd watch shows on television that he knew would give him bad dreams. It was like he wanted to make sure he had a nightmare, so he planted the seeds in his brain before he went to bed. Most nights it worked. Rather than go through the whole routine of taking him back to his room until I finally fell asleep on his floor, I let him sleep on the couch in my room. That's all he really wanted: to be near me. Before I became a dad, I valued my privacy. Now, it's not that big of a deal to me. If my son needs to be close to me, I'll let him.

I don't have room enough in this book to write about all the things I have been able to figure out and do as a dad that I never thought I could do. This doesn't make me any kind of super-dad. No, it just makes me a dad. This is what we do as parents. We find ourselves in the middle of impossible situations, and we figure something out. We don't always get it right the first time, but eventually we do. Sometimes the greatest thing we do is simply to remain calm while our children explode with emotions. We make sacrifices for our children that they are too young or too wrapped up in their own lives to appreciate, but we make them anyway. That's why all of us parents need to stop focusing on what we did wrong, fixating on our children's bad choices, and blaming ourselves for them, and start realizing that moms and dads are pretty amazing. And that includes you.

And Now a Word About the Biggest Guilt Inducer of All

I have only recently ventured into the world of parenting adult children, and even now I barely qualify since my oldest son, Anthony, graduated from high school while I was working on this book. Even my foster children who have aged out of the system are still in their early twenties, so this is new territory for me. However, I have many friends who have adult children. Over and over, I hear them say the same thing:

Your children's choices are not your responsibility.

Parents receive too much credit when a child does well and too much blame when a child crashes and burns under their own poor decisions. Kids who grew up in horrible home situations—the kind of kids you would say have no hope of any sort of a future, kids like me—those kids can turn out to be fully functioning adults with good lives. At the same time, children who grew up in the most loving homes and had the kind of childhood you see in the movies—those kids can grow up and make a complete mess of their lives. Here's the real kicker in all of this: siblings who grew up in the exact same situations turn out completely different. The same family that produces a nuclear engineer may also produce a career criminal. In fact, what inspires one child to do great things can be used by another child as an excuse for their terrible behavior. Everything comes down to the choices people make for themselves. And that's something we can influence by our example, but it's not something we can control.

So, moms and dads, stop feeling guilty over your children's choices. Instead, love them no matter what they do. Love doesn't mean approval of lifestyles. That's what makes love unconditional. And that's the most amazing thing parents do. We love no matter what. Again, it doesn't mean we always react in the right way or that we don't ever say the wrong things. We all do that, because we're humans. After all, it's not like our kids always react in the right way or never say the wrong things. That's what usually sets us off and pushes our love to the limit. But we still love them with a love that we never knew was in us until we became parents. More than anything, that's what makes moms and dads amazing.

LESSONS THAT GUIDE MY PARENTING STYLE

9

Parent a Child for Who They Are, Not Who You Want Them to Be

I grew up in a remote part of Uganda. Our village had a school, but parents had to pay for their children to attend. In a place where everyone was poor, even going to kindergarten was a luxury. Most families had to sell part of their land or perhaps a goat to make it possible. For me, this meant I went to school off and on, depending on whether my mother could find a way to pay the five or ten dollars for tuition that month. That may not sound like much, but most people in my village struggled to make a dollar a day. My father didn't care if his children received an education, but my mother did. Seeing the lengths she and my friends' families went to in order to make it possible for us to go to school reinforced the unifying truth we all knew: education was the one thing that could pave the way to a better life.

Though school always seemed just out of reach for the first fifteen years of my life, once I had the opportunity to get an education, I made the most of it . . . multiple times! When I first arrived at boarding school, I was way behind my peers. However, I worked hard not only to graduate but to finish with marks that made it possible for me to go to college. After graduating from Makerere University in Kampala, I had the opportunity to move to England to pursue a degree there. After graduating in England, I had the chance to come to the United States and get a degree there too. Again, I did whatever it took to make that happen.

The life I have now, I have because I took advantage of every opportunity and worked hard to get the best education I could. That is why, even before I became a father, I planned to instill this same drive in my children. My kids all come from hard places, just like me. The odds are stacked against them. Excelling in school is, in my mind, the great equalizer. An education will open doors and pave the way for their futures. That was my mindset going into parenthood.

Then I had kids.

And I sent those kids to school.

A few of my kids loved school, but most struggled. Because of that struggle, I nearly had to force them into the car to go to school every day. Homework became a nightly battle. I tried withholding privileges until homework was finished. Many of my children simply chose to do without rather than get their work done. That's how much they hated homework!

Clearly, I faced a dilemma. In my mind, *the* way to a better future was to get as much education as possible. It wasn't enough to finish high school. I wanted my children to get a college degree and possibly more. Our state even had a plan that basically made it possible for a child who spent time in the foster care system to go to college for free. A free college education! How could anyone turn that down?! I wasn't about to let my children miss out on something so precious and important. I had to figure out a way for my children to get over their hatred of school and apply themselves. I racked my brain, trying to come up with ways to get my children to share my dream for them. Over time, I thought I was making progress, especially with my son Stephen.

Stephen came to my home when he was sixteen. Like most kids in the foster care system, he was far enough behind in school that there was no way he'd graduate with kids his own age. However, the two of us sat down and worked out a plan for him not only to finish high school but also to possibly go on to some sort of further education, either community college or a trade school.

"Listen, Stephen," I told him time after time, "you can do this. Staying in school is your chance to build a future for yourself. The state will even pay for most of your college! This is too good of an opportunity to let slip away."

Every time we had this talk, Stephen agreed with me. He was 100 percent on board with the plan. His cooperation was crucial because he was about to turn eighteen. At that point he would officially age out of the foster care system and could make decisions for himself. However, the two of us agreed that the best plan for him was to remain a part of my family while he finished high school and whatever education followed.

Since I have included this story, you can probably guess what happened next. Immediately after his eighteenth birthday, Stephen dropped out of school and informed me he was going to go find his birth mother. He thought she lived in Baltimore. "But what about school?" I asked.

I might as well have been talking to the wall. Stephen's mind was made up. A few days later, he got on a bus and headed north. I felt like I had failed as a parent. What possible life could my son hope to find as a high school dropout? The bus might have been headed to Maryland, but I knew where it would ultimately lead, and it was not to the life I had dreamed for him.

And that was the problem. I was disappointed with my son because he was not pursuing *my* dream for him. Instead he had taken his own path, one he felt he had to go down. Stephen had spent many years in the foster care system. Like every child, he loved his mother. All he ever wanted was to be reunited with her. Now that he was eighteen, no one could keep him from doing that. I had to let him go while also letting go of my dream for him.

When Stephen headed north, I was forced to look at my expectations for all of my children. I wanted them to be good students just like I was. I wanted them to value getting as much education as possible because that's what I valued. In short, I was trying to make them become who I wanted them to be, instead of seeing them for who they were and developing the potential already in them.

The more I thought about this, the more I realized another reason I placed such a high value on education. It wasn't just that it carried me from the streets of Kampala, Uganda, to the life I now enjoy as I live out the American dream. When I asked James, the man who rescued me off the streets, why he went to all the trouble of putting me in school, he replied, "Because I can see that you have potential, Peter. You're a smart kid. I think you will do well in school."

This was the first time in my life that anyone ever saw me as something other than a dirty, smelly street kid. Everyone else I encountered saw me as human garbage, but James saw my potential even when I could not see it in myself. No wonder I loved school and went on to get multiple degrees. James saw this potential in me, and I wanted to prove him right. Isn't seeing the potential in our children what we should all do as parents?

From Negative to Positive

When I parent a child according to who I want them to be, I put unnecessary pressure on them to conform to expectations they are not made to meet. It is like someone trying to force me, at my height and age, to become a basketball star. No matter how hard I might try, I can never grow the extra foot I'd need to even have a chance, much less turn back the clock and become a young man once again. As parents, we put the same pressure on our children when we want them to become someone or something they are not.

Each one of us is created uniquely by God with our own set of gifts and abilities. For bio parents, this is especially difficult to appreciate. Our children may look like us and share many of our mannerisms. But deep down, they are not our mini-mes. Each is their own unique person. Children instinctively want to please their parents, at least at a young age. While they may say they want to do and be all the things we want them to do and be, inside they face the turmoil between being who they long to be and pleasing us. If we are not careful, our pressure for them to conform to our image can lead them to believe that our love is conditional upon their performance. Such pressure will eventually fracture our relationships with our children.

Not only will parenting children toward becoming what we want them to be put undue pressure upon them but all of our interactions will become negative. They can never live up to what we want them to be. We will constantly be pointing out where they have failed to measure up to our standards. It is like when I get on one of my children for bringing home a poor grade on a test. Berating a child for getting a D or taking away all their screen time until they bring that grade up only serves to tell them that they are not good enough in my eyes. Yes, I can be disappointed in a poor grade when the child has demonstrated over time that they can do much better, but there are ways of communicating this without causing the child to see themselves as a failure.

When we discover who our children actually are and parent them accordingly, we turn the negatives into positives. The easiest way to make this transition is to call out the positive characteristics in our children. For Stephen, it was easy for me to tell him what a mistake it was for him to drop out of school. What was much harder—but far more necessary—was for me to focus on the courage it took for him to travel to an unknown city completely on his own to go meet a woman who may or may not want to see him.

When his meeting with his mother turned sour after just a couple of weeks, he went off in search of his bio father. I know this because he called and talked to me about it. That was another thing I valued in my son. Even though he wanted to connect with his birth parents, he still valued his relationship with me as part of my family. And he has spent time back with us over the two years since he left home. Love and loyalty are valuable characteristics in my son. He is also persistent. Two years after dropping out, he walked across the stage at a school in Baltimore where he received his high school diploma. His bio mother, with whom he eventually established a good relationship, helped make that moment happen. For me, it was a double win.

Our children, however they come into our lives, are very different than we are. Once we learn who they are and parent them accordingly, being a parent becomes less frustrating. More than that, we can light our children up by seeing the potential that flows out of their unique design. That's what James did for me. He saw my potential, and that encouraged me to see it too. This is the power of what we can do for our kids when we parent them as they are, not as we hope they'll be. We give them both the confidence and the joy to grow and develop fully as the people God made them to be.

I should end on this positive note, but I need to be honest. Seeing and valuing a child's potential is easy when it is something like preferring to draw and paint instead of playing sports. The real test for us as parents comes when our children go their own way in areas that are much more important to us, like faith and sexuality. No matter how much we want our children to share our convictions, they will develop and follow their own. Eventually these convictions will come out, even if it is not until our children are adults living on their own. Parenting a child for who they are rather than who we want them to be does not stop when a child turns eighteen. It is a principle we must follow through whatever stage of parenting in which we find ourselves.

For Foster and Adoptive Parents

Our children already feel rejection from their bio parents. This makes them even more sensitive to any words that might be perceived as rejection.

Why did you get this bad grade?
You have to redo this homework and do it right this time!
Why are you so messy?
Why do you constantly lose things?
Why are you so forgetful?
Why aren't you more like your brother?

As foster and adoptive parents, we need to be even more aware of our words and our expectations. I am who I am today because a stranger saw me for who I really was. That is a gift we can also give to our children, no matter how long they might be in our homes.

10

One Size (DEFINITELY) Does Not Fit All

Obviously, children are all different. I knew this before I became a father. I knew there were differences between children of different ages. You don't parent a three-year-old like an eight-year-old nor an eight-year-old like a fifteen-year-old. Instinctively, we all know this. We all also understand there are inherent differences between boys and girls as well as children who are exploring their gender identity. As parents, we know we cannot parent all our children in the exact same way. This is especially true for me as a foster and adoptive dad, as my children come from a wide variety of backgrounds with different experiences and trauma. I must be flexible and adapt to the needs of each child to be an effective parent.

However, knowing all of this in my head did not prepare me for how extremely one size does *not* fit all. I may have expected differences between children, even between biological siblings, but sometimes the differences feel like riding a roller coaster that also jerks me around from side to side. No set of siblings threw me for a loop more than Jordan and Brad. I'd had many sibling sets before they came into my home, so I felt like I was prepared for whatever they might bring.

I should stop thinking that.

Like so many of my children, these boys came into my home angry. Again, this was nothing new. Children do not end up in the foster care system because they've experienced a wonderful childhood with the kindest, most loving parents in the safest home you can imagine. No, in the vast majority of cases, children end up in foster care because of abuse or because the parents are on drugs or in jail or dead. In other words, these children have suffered extreme trauma, and anger is one of the most common reactions to trauma. It is completely natural and to be expected.

Jordan and Brad were no exception. Both had suffered the same abuse in their bio home, and both were angry. However, each was angry for completely different reasons. Jordan was angry at his bio parents, so angry that he never wanted to see them again. The days leading up to and immediately after his supervised visits with them were the worst. He lashed out at me and everyone else in my home.

"Why do I have to see them?!" he'd scream at me. "I don't want anything to do with them. I never want to see them ever again!"

The days when his parents did not show up were the best days of his life. He was as happy as a kid opening presents at Christmas because he got exactly what he wanted. If it had been up to Jordan, we would have gone out for ice cream or something else to celebrate not having to see his parents for another month or more.

Brad, however, was exactly the opposite. He was only eight while his brother was ten, which may explain some of the differences in their reactions. Where Jordan hated his bio parents, Brad loved them so much that they were basically angels in his sight. Mom and Dad could do no wrong. He was angry much of the time he was in my house because all he wanted was to go back home. "Why can't I live with my mom and dad?" he'd cry over and over. The days leading up to visitation were a mixed bag for him. He'd get super excited, but he also did not understand why he could only have short visits with them or why someone else always had to be in the room with them. When his bio parents inevitably missed a supervised visit, it was like the world had come to an end. Brad lashed out with anger and blamed everyone else for his parents not showing up. It couldn't be their fault. He believed they had to miss him as much as he missed them. He believed they wanted him back home even more than he wanted to go himself.

I did not know what to do. Both boys had suffered the same abuse. How could their reactions be so different? My prior experience did not help me, even though this was neither my first set of siblings nor my first set of children with differing reactions to the trauma they experienced with their bio families. However, even when there had been differences in the past, I could still use the same basic road map to figure out how to help the children heal. Not with Jordan and Brad. When their bio mom or dad called, one could not wait to hear what they had to say while the other wanted no part of it. And they were both sitting there in the same room! I was in a no-win situation. Anything I did was guaranteed to set one or the other off.

What Are We to Do When Everything We Do Is Wrong?

I wish I could say that Jordan and Brad were the only two siblings to throw me onto this roller coaster. While others may not have been as dramatically opposite from one another, the differences between siblings have been great enough to leave me frustrated and exhausted. Some days I've wanted to throw my hands up in the air and just give up. If you find yourself in this place, the most important thing you can do is step back and give yourself grace. Don't feel guilty for becoming frustrated with a situation that would exasperate even the most patient person on earth. Take a deep breath, shut the kids out of your mind for a moment, and gather your thoughts.

The next step is more difficult. Parenting when one size does not fit all means we have to set aside all the assumptions we have accumulated through our parental experiences. We cannot go into a situation thinking we know exactly how we will handle it. I find it useful to remind myself that, while I may understand the experiences my children have gone through, I do not know what they feel inside. Their conflictions are their own. As an outsider, all I can do is come alongside and try to help them navigate their feelings. With Jordan and Brad, I could not help both of them in the same way. I couldn't validate what each was feeling in the same way. Each boy had to be treated as the individual they were.

For each to heal, I also had to protect the two brothers from one another at times. Doing so almost became a full-time job in itself. Everything we did together had the potential to blow up into a fight over their bio parents, even something as innocent as making crafts.

I sat down with the boys one day to draw some pictures with them. "I'm going to make something for my mom," Brad said as he grabbed some markers and went to work. He started drawing a happy picture with flowers and sunshine. Jordan looked over at his brother's picture and started making a picture for his mom as well. His? Well, the only way I can describe it is pure evil. Brad noticed, and craft time became fight time.

Once I had separated them, I pulled Jordan aside and told him that I understood how he felt, but that expressing his feelings in this way in front of his brother did not help Brad in any way. This was so hard for Jordan because he could not understand how his little brother could continue to love their parents after all they had done to them. In the same way, I did not allow Brad to take out his anger for being removed from their home on Jordan. Children always at least partially blame themselves for landing in foster care. Since Brad was happy in his bio home, it felt easy to blame Jordan for causing them to be taken away from Mom and Dad. Needless to say, craft time that day was not the last time I found myself playing the role of a peacemaker more than a parent.

Finally, when one size does not fit all, that means we must find a way to validate each of our children's feelings in a way that is effective for them. In this case, I did not punish Jordan for drawing a picture that expressed his anger. Instead, over time, I talked with Jordan about my experiences with my father. He was the first child with whom I'd ever shared so much of my story. I told him how my father had abused me and how I'd hated him for it. But I also told him that I'd realized if I continued to hate my father and stay angry with him the rest of my life, I would basically be letting my father win. He would always hold the upper hand over me. That is why, I told Jordan, I chose to forgive. It was the only way I could be free once and for all from his abuse.

While Jordan and I bonded over my story, validating Brad's feelings was more difficult because, like his brother, I didn't really understand how he could blindly love these people who had hurt him. But I couldn't let my own views get in the way of his real feelings. So, knowing what worked for one wouldn't work for the other, I found a way to meet Brad where he was too.

And that's the key for us as parents. Every child is a learning experience. Every child is so different that it's almost like starting over with each one. Yet that is also part of the adventure of raising children. We do not know what they will bring. Rather than be annoyed or angered by it, we can think of it as an opportunity to get to know them and to grow ourselves in the process.

For Parents with Blended Families

One size does not fit all, and that's especially important to remember when we blend foster kids into a family with bio kids.[2] All are children, but that's where the similarities end. Bio kids have not lived through the same trauma as their foster and adoptive siblings. They have not experienced the pain of abandonment or the trauma of having adults they have never met come and take them out of the only home they have ever known and plug them into a group of strangers. Expectations and discipline must therefore be completely different.

The same principles apply to families blended by remarriage.[3] Anytime you throw children together and tell them they are now a family, the same tensions will arise. The change is equally disruptive to both sets of children. Birth order goes out the window. Jealousy kicks in when parents' attention gets split, especially when the new kids require much more care. These problems even arise when the bio kids have all moved off to college or gotten married. The entire family dynamic is thrown for a loop.

For the parents, one thing becomes clear very quickly: you may have experience as a parent, but when you become a foster parent or adopt, you are starting over from scratch. Everything is new. Everything is completely different. If you do not appreciate this difference, if you go in thinking that the fact that you have raised three children successfully means you are ready to bring in two more who come from a hard place, you are sadly mistaken.

2. While I did not have this experience, my collaborator, Mark, did. He has three bio children and adopted two when his youngest bio child was in college.
3. Also Mark's experience from growing up in a blended family.

11

Look Beyond Behaviors to Discover Root Causes

I started to get a little concerned when George was in the bathroom for a very long time. He'd told me he needed to go, and I doubted that, at six years old, he'd decided to take a bath as well. Something had to be up. Then the smell started drifting into the living room. This kid had to be ill for the smell to be this bad.

I went up to the bathroom door and knocked. "George, are you okay, buddy?" I asked.

He mumbled something that was hard for me to make out.

"Okay, I'm coming in to check on you. Is that all right?" Again, he said something I could not understand, but the smell was also so bad that I knew I had to check on him.

As soon as I opened the bathroom door, my first instinct was to close it, leave my house, call in a hazmat team, and never return. However, as every parent knows, walking away is never an option. I not only had to leave the door open but

I had to enter the room and deal with this situation. Keep in mind, I spent five years of my life sleeping next to a dump in a city that sits on the equator. People not only dumped garbage there but also dead animals. Raw sewage flowed in a stream next to it. I still do not believe anything in this world can stink as bad as that garbage dump, but my bathroom after George smeared poop over every wall—and himself—was a close second. It was the nastiest sight imaginable. I realize that now and then a very young child with an overflowing diaper who doesn't know any better will sometimes smear poop on themselves and whatever is close to them. But George was six. And he hadn't just smeared it. It was like he'd redecorated the bathroom with it.

"What . . . what did you do?" I asked.

He didn't say anything. Instead, he just looked at me like this was perfectly normal.

I asked again. "George, why did you do this?"

"I was afraid," he said in a very quiet voice.

"Afraid? What were you afraid of, George?" I asked.

"You," he replied.

"You were afraid of me? Why were you afraid of me?" I said, confused.

"I didn't want you to hurt me."

"How did you think I might hurt you?"

George looked up at me. "I did not want you to touch me where I don't want to be touched."

My heart broke. Now I understood. "George, have other adults touched you in ways you did not want to be touched?"

He stood there, quiet, and finally nodded his head.

"I am very sorry other adults have hurt you in that way," I replied. "I promise you that you are safe here." I glanced around the bathroom. I wanted to throw up, half because of the poop and half because of how adults in George's life had sexually abused him.

"I tell you what," I continued. "Why don't you clean yourself up? I promise you that no one will come in here while you are washing." I got him some clean clothes, filled the bathtub, and then pointed at the button on the doorknob. "After you close the door, press this button. That will lock the door. Only you can unlock it. Okay?"

George nodded. I left, and he closed and locked the door. He came out a little while later fairly clean. I didn't even try to wash his poop-covered clothes. I bagged them up and threw them in the trash, which is what I wished I could do to the adults in George's life who had abused him. My heart broke for him. When an adult came after him, he was too small to fight back. Instead he had come up with his own strategy to protect himself. If he could not defeat his abusers, he could at least make sure they did not want to get close to him. And what could he use to do that? The only thing available to him: his own poop.

Now that he was in my home and away from his abusers, he was told he was safe, but for his own protection he could not allow himself to believe that. He did not know me. To him, I was just another adult who claimed they would take care of him. Other adults in his life who were supposed to take care of him had touched him in ways he never wanted to be touched again. The abuse he suffered was the root cause of his behavior. If I had punished him for what he had done, I would have only driven him further into a place of despair.

Always Ask Why

Looking for the reasons behind a child's behavior applies not only when a child acts out. Often we find ourselves completely

frustrated with our children when their behavior seems completely unconnected to the present situation. One day my daughter was extra emotional. She seemed to cry at everything, which
was not like her. When she wasn't crying, she was angry—at her
brother, at me, at the world. When I was finally able to get her
to talk to me, I asked her a very simple question.

"Are you missing your mom today?"

She nodded slowly as her eyes filled up with tears. I pulled
her close and held her.

"It's okay to miss her," I told her over and over.

In this instance it could have been easy for me not to be sym-
pathetic. Her mother had lost all parental rights for a reason.
But that didn't stop my daughter from loving and missing her
bio mother. For her *not* to miss her would have been the unusual
thing. Yet my daughter did not know how to express what she
was feeling. She may not have fully understood it herself.

I could see the root cause behind my daughter's behavior
because she had been with me long enough for me to know
her. However, with other children, especially when they are
new to my home, I have had to go into research scientist mode
and gather as much information about them as I can. Very few
children will come right out and tell us what we need to know.
Instead we must learn how to listen to them while going about
everyday life—in the car, during meals, after school. Children
will drop hints we must pick up on.

The process would be much easier for me if every kid who
comes to live in my house had a drop-down menu like a computer program that tells me all I need to know about them. But
they don't. I do not know all they have experienced both in their
bio homes and other foster homes. In many ways, I'm flying
blind. Of course, any new parent is. A crying baby doesn't stop
and tell you, "I'm crying because my diaper is wet." Figuring

that out is up to the parent. That is why we must learn as much as we can about our children through every stage of their development. Understanding the reasons behind behavior is the only way I know to keep my sanity as a parent.

Looking for root causes for behavior is also the key to understanding how to discipline a child. Effectively disciplining a child has nothing to do with punishment and everything to do with teaching and training. Our goal as moms and dads is not to produce compliant children who never act up or act out. Instead, our goal is to help them grow, learn, and mature to become emotionally and spiritually healthy adults. We can't do that by punishing behaviors without looking beyond each behavior to its root cause. This does not mean their actions do not have consequences. Yet whatever consequences they face need to also move toward teaching the child to deal with what they are feeling inside.

Only then will their behavior change.

For Foster and Adoptive Parents

Understanding the reasons behind behavior is especially important for children who come from hard places. My friend, child developmental specialist Marissa Bradford, wrote me with the following advice:

> One in four children in foster care will show signs of PTSD as a result of the events they have lived through. This means that their behavior is very often not within their control and very often related to an event that was overwhelming to their brain and body. Some behaviors that seem inappropriate may be coping mechanisms used in the midst of their previous environment to gain a sense of control over their surroundings or to self-soothe. Other behaviors are reflexive responses

generated by an overworked fear-response in the brain that keeps them on high alert for a danger that is no longer a threat. Similarly, children with PTSD may also react in extreme ways to images, sounds/ voices, or events that remind them of a traumatic event.

Outside of PTSD, children who have lived in a context of trauma may behave in disorganized or extreme ways out of habit that helped them survive in their previous context. As a foster parent, there is an opportunity to reframe some of these behaviors once the root cause is more evident. Empathizing with this root cause is the first step to taking a perspective of your child that recognizes their strengths even in the midst of behavior that seems extreme. A strengths-based or strengths-first approach allows us to see each child as an individual with unique skills and gifts. For children who have experienced trauma, resilience is a strength you can start with. For each child, the list of strengths will be different. For example, the child who continually shoplifts may be resourceful (perhaps literally, or perhaps in a sense of fulfilling the normalcy of danger that they were used to in their previous circumstance). Eventually this list of behaviors reframed as strengths can be manifested into opportunities for your child to exercise their strengths in less risky, more productive, and fulfilling ways.

12

Don't Let Your Child's Behavior Dictate Yours

Sometimes I think parenthood is really a hidden-camera game show called *When Will Mom and Dad Lose Their Minds Today?* Parents hate this game, but children love it. The rules are simple. A child or children working together must do at least one thing each day designed specifically to drive their parents crazy.

My kids play it all the time. It is like they wake up one day and say, "I wonder, will Dad lose his mind if I use every drop of hot water in the tank for one shower?" The next they say, "I wonder, will Dad lose his mind if I make all the hand soap that is supposed to last for two weeks disappear in one day?"

Another day they wake up and say, "Will Dad lose his mind if I flush an entire roll of toilet paper down the toilet?" That one has a couple of bonus questions, including "I wonder how many rolls of toilet paper it will take to completely clog the toilet," and, of course, everyone's favorite: "I wonder how many LEGOs I can flush down the toilet before it backs up."

Nearly every day they ask questions of this nature that involve going to school. These include: "I wonder, will Dad lose his mind if I don't want to get out of bed even though it is a school day and I have to get up every day at this exact time but I want to act like he has never tried to wake me up so early in my life?" "Will Dad lose his mind if I take forever to get to the car for him to drive me to school?" "I wonder, will Dad lose his mind if by the time I finally make it to the car I forgot to put on any shoes, which means he has to go back into the house to find a pair for me even though we are already running late?"

Children never run out of ways to play this game. Every parent finds themselves in one version or another nearly every day. "How many dishes can I leave on the counter before Mom loses it?" "How many lights can I leave on before Dad yells?" "How many clothes can I pile up on my bedroom floor before Mom has a meltdown?" "How many doors can I slam and how many dirty plates can I leave in the living room and how many toys can I leave scattered across the front yard before Mom and Dad have complete nervous breakdowns?" A child knows they have won when they see the sweat break out across our forehead and our eyes begin to bulge like there is a volcano inside of us until we ultimately explode and begin yelling. While it's frustrating as a parent, I have had children who considered this to be the greatest form of entertainment in the world!

Children also love to play a second variation of this game that, if it had a name, would be called *When Will Mom and Dad Cave and Give Me What I Want?* Some of my forty-two children have combined the two into one where they push me to completely lose my mind *and* give them whatever they want. Bedtime seems to be the favorite time to pull out this double game. When I say, "It's time for bed," that's the child's cue to begin screaming, yelling, crying, and using every weapon in their arsenal until I crack. "If you will stop crying, I will let you play with the iPad for fifteen minutes and then it will be time for bed," they want me to say in desperation. Many times I have done exactly that. Like any parent, especially one who is tired at the end of the day, I have found it's often easier to just give in than to fight another battle after a day filled with battles.

Another favorite time for the double game is when I try to get my children to do their homework. "You need to do your homework" is my children's cue to roll their eyes and sigh loudly or suddenly need to go to the bathroom or find themselves so hungry they could never concentrate without first eating some snacks in front of the television. It. Is. Exhausting. Again, giving in is so much simpler than fighting the homework battle again. And again. And again. In a child's mind, even if they lose today and tomorrow and the next day, they know that eventually they will wear us down. But only if we let them.

The Plan Does Not Change

In the battle of wills with our children, there are two things we must always remember. First, while this is a game for some kids, it never can be a game for us. That doesn't mean we have to be deadly serious all the time. When my kids laughed over how many rolls of toilet paper they flushed down the toilet before it finally clogged, I laughed with them. But I also handed them a plunger and told them with a smile, "Since you clogged it, you get to unclog it." I did not say this as a way of winning their game. No, I said this because every human being needs to know that actions have consequences. Clogging the toilet with every roll of toilet paper in the house needed to become a real teaching moment for my children.

We cannot think in terms of winning and losing. If we do, we cross a line from dealing with our children as our children to seeing them as our adversaries. Believe me, when there is more than one child in the home (and I've had as many as seven), we'll have days where it feels like "us against them." But those days must be the exception and not the rule.

The second thing we must always remember is that no matter how exhausted we may be or how far our children have pushed us, we are always the parents. We are the adults in the room, and we cannot act like anything less. That means keeping our emotions under control even when we want to explode at a child. We are all human, which makes this very difficult—especially when a child explodes at us. I have had children who simply lose it with me. They've stood over me and screamed at me and told me I was the worst dad in the world. It would be sooooo easy to yell back, "Well, you are the worst kid in the world who doesn't appreciate all I've done for you!" Instead, I take a deep breath and breathe a prayer that God will give me control. And when he does, I can calmly reply something like, "Ah, yes, but you still know that I am your dad." Just like that, our calm can defuse tense situations.

One of the most effective ways I have found to remain the parent even while my children do everything they can to throw me off my game is to set routines and stick with them. All my children have a set bedtime, which varies by age. I do not make a teenager go to bed at the same time as a toddler, but everyone in the household knows what time each must start getting ready for bed and when to be in bed with lights out. Each night I also give a countdown as bedtime is approaching so that its arrival will not throw my children into a screaming fit.

I also have a set time each day for homework, along with a time afterward for doing nothing but watching television, reading, or playing games. The latter is not a bribe for the former. Instead, I know that all of us need time just to chill and enjoy ourselves. While TV time is not a bribe for doing homework, it is a pretty good motivation for my kids to get their work done. My daughter who hates math will even remind me that it is time for her math homework because she wants to get it out of the way.

Setting routines works. Setting them without keeping them and giving in to my children's complaints instead does them no favors. Of course, giving in is so much easier for a parent. But that's not what we signed up for. When I became a dad, no one told me this was going to be easy. Just the opposite. I had people ask me if I had thought through my decision because parenting is one of the hardest things we will ever do, especially on the days where our kids seem determined to make it even harder for us. But the hard days are exactly what we signed up for, right? Anyone can be a child's friend. Being their mom or dad, that takes work.

Finally, no matter how far our children may try to push, we must always be quick to forgive. Paul's admonition in 1 Corinthians 13:5 that love "keeps no record of being wronged" is critical for us as parents. When we get frustrated at a child, pull out their rap sheet, and start reminding them that they did this same thing last week and we told them we weren't going to warn them again but they just don't listen, we're doing the opposite of what Paul's encouraging us to do. Even worse, we are basically telling our child that they have made absolutely zero progress. The child feels like they are just a bad kid who can't do anything right in our sight.

Instead of pulling up their past failures, I have found children are more likely to listen when we focus on today, not last week or even yesterday. Even if this is the eighty-seventh time they've been in trouble for the exact same thing, focus on today. Our frustration level screams to do just the opposite. We feel like we will explode if we don't point out how many times they have done this same thing, and WON'T THEY EVER LEARN?! Sure, we want to do that, but we can't.

We cannot allow our children's behavior to dictate our own.

For Foster and Adoptive Families

My original title for this chapter was, "Don't Let a Child's *Strange* Behavior Throw You Off Your Game." If you foster for any time at all, you will see some very, very strange behavior. When children come from a place of ongoing neglect, abuse, or stress, the way in which they see life can become warped. Behavior that is at best illogical and at worst inappropriate can be normal for them. Odd behavior can be a coping mechanism or a way of comforting themselves. I once had a child who screamed as if she were possessed by some supernatural being anytime she was left alone. I've never heard any human being scream as loud and as long and as . . . how do I put this . . . bone-chillingly as this little girl. But for her, screaming had become her survival skill after spending much of her young life completely ignored by the adults in her life. She'd be placed in a room and basically forgotten about. In response, she developed a scream no one could ignore for long. I sure couldn't! However, I also couldn't let her outward behavior dictate my response.

I only know the parental side of this equation; fortunately, Marissa Bradford generously offered me this advice:

For children who have endured trauma, automatic processes like impulse control and self-regulation are hindered by the impacts of continuous stress on the amygdala, the part of the brain responsible for our emotions and memory processing. When children struggle to control their impulses, their behavior is erratic and out of control in the eyes of a parent (and the public). The extremeness of the behavior is often outside of the child's control.

But, as the caregiver of the child, knowing the why behind these behaviors and having a plan for when they emerge is key. This plan will be unique to each child and should be considerate of the potential contexts in which the behavior might occur. The plan may be shared with the child, so they know what to expect from you, even as they might not know what to expect from themselves. Even in circumstances when the child is aware of the potential consequences of their actions, such as in situations of testing a parent or manipulating for a certain outcome, the behavior that we see may simply be the child's best effort at gaining a sense of control over their surroundings.

13

Celebrate the Small Wins

When I first signed up to become a foster dad, I requested a school-age child. As a single dad who hadn't taken care of a small child since I helped my mom with my younger siblings when I was a boy in Uganda, I did not think I could handle anyone younger than five. I wanted a child who was old enough to express themselves instead of leaving me guessing what their cries might mean. A school-age child could also do a lot of their own basic care. In other words, I would not have to change dirty diapers. As much as I wanted to be a father, I wasn't ready for diaper duty.

On top of everything else, having a child who spent at least part of their day at school would allow me to keep working my day job. Shortly after I decided to become a father, I started my own business flipping houses. I knew I couldn't keep the same work schedule as the one I had before I became a dad, but at least I'd be able to work during school hours without interruption.

Honestly, I'm having trouble typing right now because I keep laughing at how clueless I was.

On Kaine's first Monday with me, I took him to the local grade school about a mile from my house and enrolled him. I signed all the papers, met his teacher, and did everything else a parent has to do when they send their child off to school for the first time. I explained to Kaine exactly what time school let out. "I'll be here to pick you up," I said. He hugged me goodbye, and went into his classroom. I thought we were good to go until three in the afternoon.

Most parents are sad when they drop their first child off for their first day of school. Of course, most parents have been with their kids for years before that first day arrives. I was less than a week into my first stint as a parent. I wasn't sad to drop Kaine off. I was relieved because I was exhausted. Keeping up with a five-year-old is hard enough. Throw in him shattering a window with his head and that incident at Chuck E. Cheese, and I was ready for a break.

I was also anxious for Kaine to go to school for his sake. Since the moment the social worker had taken him out of the home where he was living, everything in his life had been turned upside down. His home situation was not safe for him, and even though his caregivers loved him, they could not handle him. When they contacted CPS, they honestly believed they were doing the best thing for Kaine. That's part of why my social worker thought I was the right home for him. Since I did not have any other children in my home and was a single man, I could give Kaine the undivided attention he needed.

What seemed like the best thing for the child to all the adults around him felt like losing control over everything in his life to Kaine. But school would be a familiar place, even though it was a different school than where he went before. That school was nearly two hours away. Although the teachers and the other children would be different, at least the basic setting would be the same. I honestly thought Kaine would think of it as a safe place.

Less than an hour after dropping off Kaine, my phone rang.

"We have a problem here, Mr. Mutabazi," the principal said. "Would you mind coming back over to the school."

"What did he do?" I asked.

The principal explained that, in the middle of class, Kaine tried to take a crayon from one of his tablemates. The other child said no, and Kaine flipped the table over and started screaming. "We can't get him to stop screaming, and we're afraid he's going to hurt himself or one of the other children. Nothing we've tried has worked. I hope you can get him calmed down."

I wasn't so sure I could, but I told the principal I'd be there as quickly as possible.

Over the next couple of weeks, I received a similar call nearly every day. I spent more time at the school than I did on my job sites. I often compare parenting to jumping off a cliff with no one waiting below to catch you. With all of Kaine's daily outbursts at home and at school, I felt like I was about to hit bottom. I was frustrated. He was frustrated. The school was really, really frustrated. I always told myself that I'd be an encouraging dad who saw the best in my children. In that moment, if I'm honest, I was having trouble keeping that promise to myself.

And then a miracle happened. A week passed where the school only called me three times about Kaine's behavior instead of the usual four or five. Rather than stay frustrated over Kaine still having problems at school, I decided to celebrate the small victory of the week. "Kaine, you did so much better at school this week," I told him. "I'm proud of you."

Soon we had a week where the school only called twice. We celebrated that win. When we had a week where the school only called once, we celebrated that win in a big way. It did not matter that the next week the school called three times. Three was still better than five.

My first placement taught me a lesson I've had to apply with every child who has called me Dad since. Rather than fixate on my overall expectations for my children and inevitably end up frustrated with them—and them with me—I celebrate each small, daily win. When I have a child who has a habit of stealing, I count it a victory when we go to the store and they don't take anything on that trip. I even count it a win if they do steal something but tell me about it when we get home. A child trusting me enough to be this honest with me is a huge step. It also opens the door for me to have a conversation with them about how stealing is wrong. Even then, I have the conversation on their level rather than lecture them.

Able to Breathe

Of all the lessons my children have taught me, none has been better at reducing my stress level as a dad than celebrating the small wins, especially with the daily battleground that is known as getting my kids off to school. Little did I know when I had Kaine that my frustrations connected to school were only beginning. Every school morning is a fresh battle. From getting my kids out of bed to eating breakfast to brushing their teeth to getting in the car fully dressed with two shoes on their feet, nothing is easy. Many mornings everyone in the car is in tears by the time I finally drop my kids off at the school building. The most frustrating part of it all for me is the fact that my children hate going to school so much. I can't understand it, which makes me that much more frustrated every school morning in which getting my kids to school feels like I'm dragging them off to prison.

After one particularly tear-filled morning, I stopped and asked myself what I could rejoice over that morning. I had a lot to be frustrated about, but could I find anything that even remotely looked like a win? On that morning, everyone had two shoes on their feet when they got in the car. The shoes weren't necessarily on the correct feet, but at least everyone was wearing them. It was a small victory, but a win is a win, so I chose to celebrate it. From that point forward, I counted it a win if most of my children got out of bed without yelling at me or one another. If they brushed all their teeth and did not have to change clothes afterward because they had somehow covered their shirt in toothpaste, that was a win to celebrate. If they made it to the car on time, that was a win to celebrate. Before long I could always find something to count as a sign that we were making progress.

I found choosing to focus on every small win not only reduced my own stress levels but also opened the door for me to connect with my children. Our kids can sense both our frustration and our disappointment. Celebrating the small wins puts us in a much better mood and gives us a lighter spirit with which to interact with our kids. Then, rather than constantly correcting bad behavior—or worse, pulling out that age-old parental line, "Why don't you ever . . ."—I can speak kind words toward my children that build them up rather than tear them down. When we are in constant correction mode (i.e., always telling our children what they've done wrong and what they need to improve upon), our kids feel like they can do nothing right. That's just basic human nature.

When we celebrate the wins, we enable our kids to move forward and grab more wins for themselves. Our children get to experience the feeling of real success, which increases their confidence and motivates them to strive for more. We don't have to offer some prize or take our kids out for ice cream every time they don't fail a test. Just hearing us say, "Good job, I'm proud of you," has a real psychological impact for children. By doing this we set our children up to succeed.

All of this naturally raises the question, Do we then just give up on making any real progress toward sustainable life goals for our children? Yes and no. If the goals we are trying to push our children toward by using incremental wins arise out of *our* wants and expectations for our children, then yes, we do need to give those up. Remember, one of the keys to effective parenting is to parent a child for who they are rather than who we want them to be. I cannot use celebrating all the small wins as a way to push my kids toward my goals for them. I want my children to love school and pursue as much education as they possibly can. That's *my* goal, which may not fit the ways in which my kids are wired. As a parent, my job is to help my kids discover their own way. By genuinely celebrating all the small wins along the way of them doing just that, I can help them discover their full potential. And that's a goal I will never give up on.

Is this always easy to do? Of course not! Nothing about parenting is easy. But in the end, it is all worth it, and that's what keeps us going, one small win at a time.

For Foster and Adoptive Parents

For children who come from hard places, our words of affirmation may be the first our kids ever hear. I know this from experience. When I was a boy, not only did my father abuse me physically but he also verbally tore me down every day.

You are worthless.

You never do anything right.

You are the most useless kid ever.

These were words I heard over and over again.

Too many kids in the foster care system have heard the same—or worse. Some come from homes where they experienced an even deeper form of verbal abuse: silence. Any good they did was simply ignored. No one cared if they even got out of bed in time to go to school, much less excelled. Celebrating everyday small wins with our children is our opportunity to speak life into kids who have never heard such words before. I know this both as a child and as a parent: words of life will produce life inside a child. They did for me, and they do for my children.

14

Children Are Really Good at Self-Sabotage

Self-sabotage is all about control. I know this from experience. The streets of Kampala taught me that every good thing would eventually turn bad. It might take a week, two weeks, maybe even a month or more, but no good thing stayed good for long. That is why, in my mind, it was better not to wait for the inevitable but instead take control and make it happen now. Whenever someone showed me kindness, I always ultimately paid a price for it. Therefore, rather than wait for someone to disappoint me, I'd do it myself. If someone gave me a shirt and told me how nice it looked on me, I knew they had ulterior motives. Instead of waiting for them to come and collect, I'd throw the shirt away. Every time I felt myself getting close to someone who told me they liked me, I always believed they were lying to me. The one way I could keep them from lying again was to wreck the relationship and put distance between us. It didn't matter how much my actions hurt me. Hurting myself was better than allowing someone else to hurt me.

I almost flunked out of boarding school because of my self-sabotage. I was a good student. When my teachers noticed and complimented me for it, I knew they had to be lying. *What do they really want?* I asked myself. Whatever it was, I decided I'd spoil it before they could collect. So I let my grades fall. Of course, my actions made no sense. My teachers were simply trying to encourage me, especially since I had not been in school in more than five years, but I could not see that at the time. No good thing in my life stayed good for long, and it was better not to wait. I could cause the inevitable to happen right then. At least that way, I was in control.

Of course, deep regret, self-doubt, and self-loathing always followed. Always. *Why did I do that? I made a huge mistake! I am so stupid. I am the worst person in the world! How could I do that to this person who was only trying to be nice to me? That's it. I've blown it. Things will never be the same. They're going to hate me now, and I don't blame them because right now I hate myself. I don't deserve anyone ever doing anything for me ever again.* I wallowed in my regret—until time passed and someone else invited me to eat dinner with them or gave me a gift or committed some other unthinkable act of kindness. Then I automatically jumped right back into the cycle of self-sabotage followed by regret and self-doubt and self-loathing and punishing myself. This cycle kept chewing me up until I finally matured to a place where I realized what I was doing to myself. (And yes, therapy also helped!)

Thirty years after I was that street kid, I became a dad. My son Stephen was close to turning eighteen and had never learned how to drive. He was old enough for a driver's license when he came to live with me, but no one had ever made the effort to help him get one. I decided I'd give this gift to my son. I found a driving school near our home, paid to enroll him, and offered to drive him there for his first day of class. I thought I was doing something good for him, but he didn't exactly respond like I was doing him any favors.

"Who do you think you are, enrolling me in driving school without asking me first?!" Stephen yelled, punctuating every word with an f-bomb. "You aren't my dad. You can't just do that!"

I was taken aback. What had I done wrong? I thought every kid his age wanted to get their driver's license.

"Wait, wait, wait," I said. "Don't you want to learn to drive?"

"That has nothing to do with it! If I want to learn how to drive, I'll learn how to drive! I don't need you to make that decision for me!"

"Okay, okay," I said. "You don't have to go to driving school. No one is going to make you learn to drive." I did not push the matter because I knew it would not do any good. When I was Stephen's age, I would have reacted in the exact same way.

A few days later, after Stephen had cooled down, I brought the subject up again. "I know I made you mad when I enrolled you in driving school without your permission," I said, "but I had a reason. I know your girlfriend lives five miles away. I thought you might want to drive there yourself or even go on dates without me having to chauffeur you. You've also talked about getting a job. I thought it might be nice for you to be able to drive to work instead of depending on someone to drop you off and pick you up. That's all I was thinking. I did not mean any disrespect by signing you up. I just thought that a driver's license might help you enjoy life a little more."

Rather than blow up again, Stephen looked at me and said, "I didn't mean to get mad at you. It's just that, when you told me about driving school, I felt it was too good to be true. No one had ever done anything like that for me before, so why should you, you know? I really didn't feel like I was worthy of something so nice."

For the first time, I understood how my teachers at my boarding school in Uganda, as well as all the adults in my life who had tried to help lift me up, had felt.

So, What Can We Do?

The range of a child's self-sabotage knows no limits. I've seen them not eat their favorite meal I've cooked for them because they did not believe anyone would do something so nice for them. I've had them yell and scream and curse at me as if they were genuinely trying to drive me out of their life because they did not believe anyone could love them unconditionally. Driving me away on their terms was easier for them than waiting for me to abandon them like everyone else in their life had. I've seen my children fail tests even when they were prepared and quit teams even though they were good enough to play and do just about anything a person could do to hurt themselves and their future for no good reason.

I wish I could give you a simple formula that will make self-sabotage disappear from our children's lives. I wish I had a way to convince my children to believe in themselves enough to try new things and push through when working toward a goal gets hard instead of just giving up to avoid the disappointment of failing. I wish I knew the secret of getting children to trust me enough to really believe I only want the best for them when I do something "wrong" like sign them up for driver's ed. The only thing I know to do is to stay consistent with my children and, in the words of the apostle Paul, "not get tired of doing what is good. At just the right time we will reap a harvest of blessing if we don't give up" (Gal. 6:9).

Pointing out how a child is only hurting themselves in the middle of a full-blown self-sabotage incident only makes things worse. Instead, I've learned it is best to wait until they've cooled down and are probably in the middle of the regret, self-doubt, and self-loathing phase of the cycle. Then, I engage them in an open conversation. I know from experience that no one can lecture a child out of anything, much less a lifestyle of self-sabotage. Nor can all my reassurances that "You've got this" or "You can do anything you set your mind to" heal the wounds that bring on this behavior. Instead, I try to get my child to open up about why they just threw away the toy they had begged for. I do this by staying completely calm and not showing any signs of frustration. It's not easy, because watching a child sabotage their own life can make me lose my mind. I keep those feelings to myself and instead ask a question like, "I noticed you threw the bike I got for you into the trash. May I ask why you trashed it?"

"I didn't want it," my child will say.

"I understand that, and believe me, that's okay with me. But I also noticed that when you came to live with me, you really watched all the other kids on their bikes and mentioned wanting one yourself. What made you change your mind?"

"I just did."

"Okay. That's okay. But here's what I am going to do. I am going to take the bike out of the trash and keep it in the garage. If you ever change your mind, it is there for you. If you don't, that's okay. The bike will be there if you want it."

"I won't change my mind. I don't want a bike. I don't even know how to ride one."

At that point, my child reveals exactly why they threw their bike away: no one had ever taught them to ride one. They would rather throw the bike away than admit that. I then offer to help them learn to ride, an offer they usually accept. It's not that I haven't offered before. I buy a bike for every child who comes into my home. When I do, I also offer to teach them to ride, but that offer is on my terms. When it comes on the child's terms, they are more open to receiving it.

Again, self-sabotage is often a form of control for kids who feel like they have no control over anything else in their lives. We can't expect them to surrender that control to us just because something is good for them or is in their long-term best interests. Kids, especially those who come from a place of trauma, do not think long-term. That is why it is important for us to create safety in their relationship with us. Fear drives self-sabotage, but trust can build a bridge over it.

For Foster and Adoptive Parents

On top of every other factor that drives kids to sabotage themselves, many come from homes where self-destructive habits are the norm. Children may have never had an adult in their lives who has overcome obstacles to reach a goal or who has encouraged them to do their best. We might then think that kids from hard places would immediately respond to our positive words and examples, like a starving person walking into a fully stocked pantry. We might think that, but we would be wrong. I have had children come into my home knowing nothing but food insecurity, children who see snacks on the counter and a refrigerator filled with good things to eat, children for whom I cook anything they tell me they want. Those same children then struggle with eating anything at all. It's not just that the sudden availability of food is overwhelming. The reason often goes back to why Stephen cursed me out when I tried to take him to driving school: these kids don't feel worthy of having food. Constant hunger feels normal to them. And normal equals safe.

Of course, children don't come out and say these things, but you can see it on their faces when they try to force food into their mouths. Nothing is so frustrating to a parent. "Why won't you eat?!" I've asked over and over, but that only makes the situation worse. The child doesn't know the answer. They cannot put the reasons for their self-sabotage into words, and they feel ashamed by it. But that doesn't have to be the end of the story.

I did not start to trust people enough to accept an act of kindness until I was in my mid-twenties. Even today, I battle a knee-jerk reaction inside myself to pull away from those who get close to me and to sabotage the relationship before they can disappoint me. I've learned how to manage these tendencies. Our children can as well. As parents, the best thing we can do is remain patient and give them both the time and space to come around—on their terms.

15

Acting Out Can Be a Sign of Trust

I never worry when a child comes into my home and has a massive meltdown within the first twenty-four hours. Being removed from a home and dropped into a family of strangers is unbelievably stressful and traumatic, and acting out in response to stress and trauma is normal, not just for children but for every human being. How many couples get into arguments over things that do not matter at all because one or both had a stressful day at work? Stress plus trauma is an explosive combination. That's why I never worry about a child who acts out as soon as they arrive in my home. In fact, I expect it.

However, I do worry when a child from a hard place arrives in my home and is a complete angel for a week, or two weeks, or a month, or more. Angelic behavior is not normal, not just for a child who has experienced trauma but for any child. A seven-year-old boy in the most stable, loving, perfect family cannot go a week without acting out. Most seven-year-old boys cannot go an entire day without doing something that gets them in trouble. That's because they are seven-year-old boys! But I have had children come into my home and not do anything out of line for so long that I start to wonder if this is a child or a robot. The longer they hold on to their angelic behavior, the more amazed I become. The energy it takes for a child to bottle up their feelings for weeks must be incredible. I don't know how they do it, but I know why. A child keeps everything bottled up because they are afraid if they show me who they really are, I will kick them out.

Eventually, the inevitable happens. The angel disappears and is replaced by an atomic bomb (only more destructive!). The seven-year-old boy who yesterday got up on time and came downstairs for breakfast already dressed for school now comes in like the Tasmanian Devil. He yells at me. He yells at his brothers and sisters. He refuses to eat his favorite cereal because he now hates it. When I ask what is wrong, he curses at me with a vocabulary no seven-year-old should have ever heard, much less use. Getting him into the car to go to school is only slightly easier than bringing peace to the Middle East. After I drop him off at school, I already know I will be back. I make sure my phone is turned up so that I will hear it when the school calls to tell me there's been an issue with my child. The longer my child has bottled up his emotions since arriving at my home, the sooner in the day I know the call will come. Sometimes I wonder if I should just park in the school lot rather than waste my time driving home.

Most people who become foster parents give up their license within the first year, and this is part of the reason why. When the explosion comes, they are unprepared. They mistake the angelic behavior of the first few weeks for the real child. Not only are they unprepared for the child acting out in ways they never expected (but should have) but these parents also jump to the mistaken conclusion that they have done something wrong, as if their "bad parenting" brought on the change in the child's behavior. They take the child lashing out at them as rejection or a sign of their failure. Their guilt gets even worse when they go out in public as a family—and the child goes back to being an angel around strangers at a restaurant, or church, or the community pool. But as soon as they get home, the Tasmanian Devil is back. When the acting out keeps on, and on, and on, no matter what they do, these parents eventually give up. *We're not doing this child any good*, they conclude, *so he should go to a family that can help him.*

But here's the truth: a child acting out at home is actually a sign that they trust you. It's an indication they feel safe enough to let their true self come out. That angelic child disappearing and becoming a heat-seeking missile just looking for a reason to blow up at you is not a sign that you have done something wrong as a parent. Just the opposite. You have earned their trust. They feel safe with you and in your home. Now they can let out all the emotions and hurt and pain they've kept bottled up inside. Before, they were testing you. Their acting out is a sign that you have passed the test.

And Now for the Hard Part

I think I speak for everyone when I say that when someone yells and curses at me and tells me they hate me and that they cannot wait to get away from me and slams their fists into the wall because they are so angry at me for no reason, I instinctively want to respond in a way that will make this behavior stop. Telling me that their screaming at me that I'm the worst father in the world is actually a sign that they trust me is not exactly good news right then. I need them to stop yelling. I don't like to be verbally abused. No one does. I don't enjoy having a child throw a tantrum and try to hit their brothers and sisters. My other kids don't enjoy that either. I can tell myself that the child is only doing this because they feel safe enough in my home to be vulnerable and express how they feel, but, honestly, it's a lot more peaceful in the house when they feel a little less safe and stay bottled up. Of course, remaining bottled up is not healthy for anyone.

So, what do we do when our children act out, especially when their behavior comes from stress, trauma, or disappointment? Keep in mind, a child does not have to come from a hard place to experience all these things. The loss of a pet can lead to a child acting out because they have no other way of expressing their grief. A friend moving away can be the trigger, as can the end of the school year where now they don't get to spend time with all their friends. I am not suggesting we simply chalk up all bad behavior to some level of trauma and let it go at that. Acting out needs to be addressed. The question is this: How can we do it in a way that helps the child move to the other side of their trauma?

Empty threats and knee-jerk, reactionary punishments come naturally, but they are not the answer. I've never had a child who looked at me and said, "Oh, I will never do that again," when I threaten to ground them for six months for repeatedly cursing at me. And me yelling, "Don't you speak to me like that, young man! I am your father!" has never made one of my children stop and say, "Oh my gosh. I did not realize I was showing disrespect to you, Father dear. I will never do that again." We all know this, and yet in the heat of the moment, when it feels as though we are engaged in a death-match in a battle of wills, words like these have a way of coming out. We've all been there. Don't punish yourself.

Punishment itself is also not the answer. Actions should have consequences, but for most of my kids, as well as most children who have come through the foster care system, much of their abuse was labeled "punishment" by their abusers. That was my experience as a boy. My father beat me mercilessly for doing something as small as not fetching his cigarettes fast enough. He wasn't trying to teach me anything except how to hate him, and teaching is at the heart of discipline. The moments when a child melts down are teaching moments. The fact that they now trust us enough to let this behavior out means they are open to learning from us . . . if we do it in the right way.

Teachable Moments, Not Time for Punishment

Teaching through discipline begins with learning to listen to what a child is expressing through their behavior. In other words, we must listen to hear the root cause. Don't expect to find that answer quickly or easily. The roots of trauma are deep. They do not immediately reveal themselves. However, as we patiently listen and interact with a child, they will tell us stories along the way that will give us insight into what is going on in their minds. Of course, there are times when the root cause has nothing to do with trauma. When a teen abuses porn on their smartphone, it may not be because they were sexually abused. It may just mean the hormones raging in their body want to look at porn.

The second key is to find consequences to their actions that will teach without making the feelings of trauma inside even worse. Many kids who come from hard places have experienced a lifetime of rejection. Therefore, if I send them up to their room for an extended time-out, I am reinforcing that pattern. On top of that, neglected kids are used to being alone all the time. "Go to my room?" they say. "Sure. No problem." Being alone is normal for them, which is why I do the opposite. Instead of sending a child off to their room to be alone, I tell them they must stay right beside with me while I fix dinner, clean the house, or whatever it is I have to do. By doing this, I communicate that I am not going to reject them, but I am also going against what they consider to be normal. What kind of consequence is it to make a child stay with you? All I can say is come spend some time in my house. Believe me, many of my kids don't want to be sentenced to helping Dad with dinner. They'll stop doing whatever it is they need to stop doing in order to escape it.

I also find it important to talk with my children after their blowup has passed and calm has returned. When a child feels safe enough to let their true feelings come pouring out, they trust you. Build on that trust by having a back-and-forth conversation about what they are feeling. It can be as simple as asking them why they acted the way they did.

I have had sets of siblings where the older sibling basically filled a parental role for the younger sibling before they came to me. Children as young as four or five do this. It's part of their surviving together and being there for one another. However, once the children come into my home where I am now the dad, the older child can struggle with letting go of control of their little brother or sister. It gets worse when the little brother or sister figures out that they no longer have to do what their bigger sibling says. Dad's in charge now. For me, this is a very special kind of teachable moment. I don't get on the older children for trying to look out for their siblings. This is a strength in them that needs to be praised. Instead, we will talk about what life was like before and how it can be going forward. Again, this comes from a place of trust—of them toward me and me toward them.

Only when children fully trust us will they allow themselves to become vulnerable. We need to reward that trust and build on it. Only then can we help them move beyond trauma to the life they desire.

16

Children Have to Learn to Make Their Own Choices and to Live with the Consequences

Waking up a teenager on a school morning is the absolute worst. They grunt and yell and complain and basically destroy your day before it even gets started. The teen also objects that waking them up in the morning, along with telling them when they have to be in their room and quiet at night, is treating them like a baby. I can't change the fact that they must be quiet in their room by a certain time at night because I often have young children whom I need to stay asleep once I've finally gotten them down for the night. Trying to convince a toddler they need to go to sleep is only slightly less frustrating than waking a teen in the morning. I can't change the former, but I can deal with the latter.

After one of my sons complained enough about me waking him up in the morning, I finally told him, "Set your own alarm, and get up when you want. But we leave for school at the same time. If you are not up and ready to go, that's on you."

"Sure," he agreed, and probably added something like, "Finally!"

"However," I continued, "if you are not downstairs and ready to go when I have to leave to take your brothers and sisters to school, I will leave without you."

"Okay. How will I get to school, then?"

"I'll still take you, but on my time. I'm not going to turn my schedule upside down to cover for you if you oversleep."

"Sure," my son said, happy with this agreement. "That's great."

"So we have a deal?" I asked.

"Deal."

My son felt like he'd been set free from me, but I was really the one who was free—from his grumpy morning routine. However, my son's joy over his newfound freedom did not last long. One morning he either slept through his alarm, forgot to set it, or thought he hit the snooze button but instead turned it off. However it happened, he was nowhere in sight when I left to take all my kids to school. By the time I got home, he was downstairs waiting for me.

"I overslept," he said.

"I thought so," I replied.

"So, I'm going to need you to take me to school."

"Of course," I said, "but I already have something scheduled for right now. I will take you when I can."

My son didn't argue. He didn't yell at me. He didn't pace around like a caged animal, sighing loudly to let me know that he needed to leave as soon as possible. He didn't do any of that because he knew I was going to take him to school on my time, not his. He'd agreed to my terms when I told him he was responsible for getting himself up every morning. I wasn't going to change now just because he was going to be very late for school. He knew this, which was why, instead of making a big deal of my not dropping everything to get him to school, he just sat and waited quietly.

Eventually I finished whatever it was that I was doing (which honestly probably wasn't anything important) and said, "Are you ready to go?"

"Yep," he said, without complaining. He also did not complain on the way to the car or during the drive to school. I think he'd missed at least one class by the time we got there. I did not walk with him to the school office to get a pass for being tardy. That was his responsibility, since it was his choice that made him late. I could have gone in and made some excuse for him, but if I had, what would my son have learned? As a dad, teaching my son to handle life in the real world is my top priority. Once he's out of my house and on his own, I won't be there to make sure he gets up in time for work, nor will it be my responsibility to smooth things out with his boss if he oversleeps and gets to work late.

From the time a child becomes mine, my primary goal is to help them become a confident, independent, self-sustaining adult. Hovering over a child all the time to make sure they do what they are supposed to do when they are supposed to do it—or plowing the road in front of them to make sure they never have to face adversity or consequences from their poor choices—will not do them any favors. There comes a point where every child must learn to make their own choices and live with the results. And the sooner in their lives that we begin the process of letting them do just that, the better.

It's not like we have a lot of choice. Human beings assert their will and resist being told what to do long before they are old enough to talk. I did not understand how early the quest for control hits until I had a ten-month-old girl placed in my home. At the time of this writing, she has been with me for two years. Some days I think she's the one in charge and the rest of us are just living in her world. I don't have to guess what she is doing or what she wants because she lets me know beyond a shadow of a doubt. I never realized how a toddler can turn your world upside down, but she does.

Obviously, this toddler does not know what is best for her. No child of any age fully does. However, rather than try to crush my little girl's will and force her to conform to mine, I find ways to give her a degree of control over her own life while also protecting her. I don't let her choose to do whatever she wants, or eat whatever she wants, or wear whatever she wants, but I do give her two or three choices to choose between. This gives her some semblance of control and choice, even at a young age.

As my kids get older, their level of responsibility for their choices increases. I do not go into their closets and pull out two or three clothing choices for the day. Instead, I let them choose what they will wear based on what is going on that day. They know we wear church clothes to go to church, school clothes to go to school, and play clothes during the summer when they're going to spend a lot of time outside.

Since my kids are kids, they don't always make wise choices, especially in late fall and early winter. Every year, I tell my children that it is cold outside, so they need to wear something warm. And every year, one of them (such as my eight-year-old son) comes downstairs ready for school wearing a short-sleeved T-shirt.

"Hey, buddy," I say, "you know it's cold outside today. You should probably wear a sweater instead of a T-shirt."

"I know it's cold, but I don't want to wear a sweater," he pops back.

"You can wear what you want, but if you dress like that you are going to get cold because it will be cold all day long." I try to avoid using a dad voice when I say this. Instead, I use a conversational tone to spell out the consequences. Then I always follow with asking, "So, is this the shirt you want to wear?"

"I'll be okay."

"Okay, then," I tell him. "That's your choice. However, you know the rule. There's no complaining about being cold."

"I know, Dad," my son says in a way that always includes an eye roll even when he doesn't roll his eyes.

Whether it is wearing a T-shirt on a cold day, or buying a scooter, or whatever the choice might be, I try to have a conversation like this in which my child and I discuss their options and the consequences of each one. Then we agree on their choice. After all, the choice is theirs—and so is the outcome. I allow them to take responsibility for both their choice and what they need to do going forward. When a decision goes bad, like my son wearing a T-shirt instead of a sweater on a cold day and shivering all the way to school and back, I do not lambaste them with a bunch of I-told-you-sos. Instead I make my son a cup of hot chocolate to help him warm up. I also smile a lot the next day, when the weather is just as cold and he chooses to wear a sweater.

Consequences make great teachers.

Character Is Formed Through Adversity

Now, some of you reading this may be shaking your heads and thinking that I'm not a very good father if I let my son go out on a cold day wearing a flimsy T-shirt. There are those who think I should force my child to wear what I tell him to wear for his own good. But is making him dress warmly when he is adamant that he wants to wear a T-shirt really for his own good? I don't think so. I do not have to have this conversation with the same child more than once. After freezing all day, they nearly always choose to wear something warm the next time I tell them it is cold outside. The lessons we learn through suffering consequences of our poor decisions have a way of sticking with us much longer than falling in line with someone's rules without thinking. On top of that, the stronger I object to my son wearing a T-shirt on a cold day, the more he will want to wear it. That's also human nature. I find it better for my son in the long run to let him make his choice and learn from it. The more I can do this with small choices, the better equipped my children will be for the big choices that wait down the road for them.

This style of parenting is actually the way in which God parents us. Romans 5:3–5 puts it this way:

> We can rejoice, too, when we run into problems and trials, for we know that they help us develop endurance. And endurance develops strength of character, and character strengthens our confident hope of salvation. And this hope will not lead to disappointment. For we know how dearly God loves us, because he has given us the Holy Spirit to fill our hearts with his love.

God loves us, but he does not shield us from problems or trials, especially not those of our own making. Instead, he uses our problems to develop endurance and strength of character. In other words, *maturity*. That's God's goal for us. He wants to make us mature and complete, lacking nothing in terms of the character we need to shape us into the people he created us to be (James 1:5).

My life shows how true this is. I have many painful memories from my life, but I would not be the man I am today without them. In fact, if I had not experienced life on the streets and the pain of rejection from my own father, I would not be able to relate to my children who come from hard places. There's a very good chance I never would have become a foster dad at all. While I wish I had not experienced my pain, in the end, it has made me a better man and a better father.

Allowing our children to take the lead in their own lives, even when the consequences are negative, sets them up to learn and to grow. Through it, they learn decision-making while improving their judgment. Making their own decisions and learning from the bad ones builds their confidence. It makes children more resilient. One of the greatest lessons any of us can ever learn is that failure is not fatal. Because our kids live in a messed-up world, they will fail. They will go through hard times. However, when we allow them to learn how to deal with both early in life, they'll be better equipped as adults when life goes off the rails.

For Foster and Adoptive Parents

We face a greater challenge with our children who come from hard places. Trauma stunts our children's emotional development. While they may be fifteen or sixteen years old physically, emotionally they may still be only eleven or twelve. Often a child will play with toys below their age almost as a way of regaining part of the childhood that was stolen from them. I am not surprised when a fifteen-year-old girl plays with Barbies, hangs on to stuffed animals, or loves on a doll like a much-younger child. This is part of her healing process.

In terms of choices, we must be very aware of our children's emotional maturity when discerning the level of responsibility to give them over their own lives. It's a delicate balancing act.

On the one hand, they will remind us of their age and what they should be able to do. On the other hand, giving them too much of the lead in their lives often ends in disaster. Where do we find the middle ground between giving them space to grow in their maturity while also allowing them to heal without compounding the trauma they've already experienced with more failures today? I wish I had an easy answer. The hard truth is that we have to navigate this with lots of grace and lots of patience for our kids. That's the only way!

SECTION 3

LESSONS SPECIFICALLY FOR FOSTER AND ADOPTIVE PARENTS

17

We Chose This Life, Our Children Did Not

When I made the decision to become a foster parent, I turned my life upside down to get ready. The condo where I lived in Denver was great for a single man but not a family. If I was going to become a dad, I had to buy a larger house. Large family homes in Denver are quite expensive. That was going to be a problem because I knew I also had to change jobs. My job required me to be on the road most of the time, both in the United States and abroad. I could not continue to travel for weeks at a time and be a single dad, but I could not stop traveling and keep that job.

In short, everything had to change.

I ended up moving to Oklahoma City, which had a lower cost of living. I also started working for a contractor rehabbing rental houses, which ultimately led me to start flipping houses.

Changing jobs and moving were just the first steps on the road to becoming a foster dad. Those of you who have gone down this same road know what came next. After I became established in my new job, I started going through background checks and character reference checks, on top of taking hours upon hours of classes, watching training videos, reading all sorts of books, and completing all of the other steps to become a licensed foster parent. At the same time, I bought a house and completely re-modeled it to make sure everything in my home matched all the CPS foster parent home guidelines. Of course, after my first home study I had to make further changes until everything was exactly the way it needed to be for a child to come live in my home.

But I still was not through with the preparations. I had to now get myself ready spiritually, emotionally, physically, and financially. Getting ready to become a single dad in my forties, after living on my own basically since I was a young boy, put me on my knees praying more than I had ever prayed before. I also went through a lot of soul-searching, wondering if I was up to this task. Even after I did everything I needed to do to be approved for my license, I kept reading more and more books, watching online seminars, and basically trying to overprepare for my first placement.

Judging by what I've shared about my first placement, you already know that no matter how prepared I thought I was, I wasn't prepared enough. Once Kaine had gone to sleep those first nights, I spent my evenings reading more and going back over my training to find even more resources to help me survive parenthood. I chose this life, and I wanted to make sure I did everything I could to live it well, both for myself and for my kids.

Alien Abduction

Our kids, on the other hand, have exactly zero preparation before they are thrown into the foster care system. Some adult they do not know shows up at wherever the only family they have ever known happens to be living. The next thing the kids know, some of their clothes and toys are thrown into a black garbage bag before they are led outside to a waiting car. No one asks the kids if they want to get in the car; they don't have a choice. Their parents may be crying, yelling, or, worse yet, not doing anything at all. The kids are almost always crying, especially if this is their first time to be taken from their home. The adult the children does not know tells them something about going to a new, safe home, but the kids are in shock. They do not understand what is happening to them. Then the car arrives at a strange house, a child welfare office, a police station, or a Walmart parking lot. The adult the kids do not know introduces them to another complete stranger who is now supposed to take care of them. Again, no one asks the kids if they want to stay with this stranger, and once again, they do not have a choice. The stranger shows the kids where they will now sleep and where they will eat, and while he or she tries to be nice, all the kids can think about is how much they want to go home.

A child's experience of being thrown into foster care feels a lot to them like an alien abduction, and we, the foster parents, are the aliens! And the aliens do everything different.

Different nighttime routine.

Different bath time routine.

Different morning routine.

Different mealtime routine.

Nothing is familiar to the children.

The alien's house smells different from any house the kids have lived in. The language they use is different, or at least the way they speak it without yelling, and screaming, and streams of profanity is! The alien's food is different. Green stuff shows up on plates along with something these aliens call fruits and vegetables. For a lot of the kids, this is a food group they did not know existed. The alien's home is usually much, much quieter with far fewer people inside. Some of our kids have come from homes where people abused drugs or had sex right in front of them. That's the only normal they've ever known. Now they've come to a house where no one does anything like that. The kids don't know why. They don't know anything about this strange home and these strange people with whom they are now supposed to live.

If you were in our children's position, how would you react to your own alien abduction? How about your second alien abduction? Or your third? Some of our kids go through this ten times or more before they finally age out of the system. No one offers them classes on how to succeed in foster care, and even if they did, our kids probably wouldn't think they are going to be in the system long enough to need them. Most just want to go home, and in my experience, most believe their moms and dads are doing everything they can to get them back.

This *Is* What We Signed Up For

Our kids did not sign up to be thrown into the foster care system, but these are exactly the kids we signed up for when we decided to become foster and adoptive parents. It is easy for us to forget this. We knew we would be getting children who had been removed from their biological homes for whatever reason. That's the definition of foster care. However, for a lot of us, at least in the beginning of our journey, we did not expect kids like these—kids living through the trauma of an alien abduction. We understand they come from trauma. No child is removed from their home because their life there is so wonderful. In our minds, we understand these are children from hard places, but it is easy for us to forget that being placed in our homes is another form of trauma—one that is in our children's faces all day, every day.

That is why when we say something like, "Son, your dinner is ready," the child will snap, "I'm not your son," or, "Don't call me that. I already have a dad, and you are not him!" It is also why our kids often do not appreciate the room we took so much time decorating. Instead they turn up their noses as if we're forcing them to live in a garbage dump. This is true even if the kids come from a house filled with literal garbage! Garbage feels normal. Clean and new seem somehow threatening.

The trauma of being stuck in a stranger's home is also why our children treat what we treasure like trash. It is why they pull back when we try to show them any sort of basic kindness. In their eyes, we are just an extension of the adults who pulled them out of their home, and that's how they are going to treat us. Not all children do this, but enough do that we'll find ourselves in the middle of a figurative five-alarm fire as every one of the worst-case scenarios they warned us about in our training classes comes true.

We were told these children would lie to our faces even when it is easier for them to tell the truth, and yet we still are shocked when a child lies to our face. We were told these children would reject our attempts to connect with them, and yet we are shocked when, no matter what we try, they push us away. We were told these children would be on edge, and the slightest thing would set them off. And again, we were still surprised when the slightest thing set them off. I receive messages from parents who live with all these alarms going off day in and day out. They tell me they don't know what to do, even though these are the situations our training was trying to get us ready to handle. Even worse, I often hear, "I didn't sign up for this!" My friends, this is exactly what we signed up for.

I understand feeling overwhelmed. However, we must never forget that we signed up for this. Our children did not. We trained for these exact situations, but our children were never offered classes on how to survive foster care. We had time to prepare ourselves, while our children were thrown into this. Because we were the ones trained, because we were the ones who volunteered for this duty, it is up to us to take the lead in helping our children survive and hopefully thrive in our homes. Getting to that point will take a lot of time, but again, that's what we signed up for.

The question, again, is this: How do we do it?

Early on in my foster parent journey, I had a social worker explain to me the different roles I was now taking on. I thought I was just a dad, but she told me I had also signed up to be a police officer, a detective, an emergency therapist, a counselor, and a mediator between my kids and their bio parents. The role I fill at any given moment depends on the situation. I am always Dad, but from the moment a child comes into my home, I must begin an investigation to help me understand this child and why they do what they do. When I first became a dad, I asked my kids questions and believed all their answers. A lot of times I found myself wondering how they ever ended up in foster care because the life they described sounded incredible. They talked about a nice house, and a yard, and a mom or dad or both who loved them. In the end, though, it didn't take much detective work to know they were lying.

Also, many of the kids who come into our homes want to please us. They not only put on their best behavior but also tell us what they think we want to hear. Again, a little digging shows they are lying. Then we must turn into a counselor and therapist to help understand why they are lying. Throw in the visits with bio parents, and we not only have to mediate between our children and them but are the ones left to try to help our kids come through their grief and anger when the parents don't show up. This job gets even more difficult because the child usually takes their anger out on us.

Again, this is what we signed up for when we became foster and adoptive parents. We signed up to become moms and dads to kids who don't want us to be their moms or dads. We signed up to provide a safe environment for kids who think chaos is normal. We signed up to be there for children from hard places who have nowhere else to go. We did not sign up to do this because we expected any show of appreciation from them or from anyone else. How can we expect our kids to be grateful for what we do when they don't want to be in this predicament? It's like ordering a huge barbecue meal with every kind of meat, having it sent as a surprise to a family of vegans, and expecting a huge thank-you in return.

As foster parents, we should not expect anything back from our kids.

We signed up to love them unconditionally; they did not sign up to love us back.

We signed up to provide a safe home for them; they did not volunteer to come live with us.

We signed up to give and give and give as parents; they did not sign up to become our children.

We signed up to parent selflessly. How our children respond will differ from child to child. In fact, they don't have to respond at all. We didn't sign up to do this for their response. We signed up to be a foster parent or to adopt a child because we chose to do so. Any response in kind from a child is just icing on the cake.

18

The Roots of Trauma Do Not Magically Disappear

I had barely made it to my hotel in Seattle when my phone rang. My dad-sense kicked in, sort of like Spider-Man's spidey-sense, and I knew something was wrong before I even answered the phone. "Hello," I said in that quick way that really means, *What happened?!*

"Peter, Anthony is sick," the friend who was keeping my son while I spoke at a conference replied.

"Really?" I was confused. "He was fine when I left a few hours ago."

"He's running a fever and throwing up. He can't keep anything down. He has a headache and just feels terrible all over. I don't know. It could be the flu or some stomach bug that's going around. It's hard for me to do much for him because he just keeps saying, 'I want my dad. I want my dad.'"

Anthony first asked if he could call me "Dad" the day he was placed in my home. I told him no, but that lasted for all of twenty minutes. I wasn't being mean by telling him no. Instead, I was trying to protect my heart. I had just come off a very emotional goodbye to two children for whom I had been a dad for nine months. At one point my social worker told me their parental rights were about to be terminated, which would open the door for me to adopt them and be their forever father. But a judge made a different decision and sent my children to live with a blood relative, leaving me heartbroken and unsure if I could foster again. I'd planned to take at least three months off before even considering another placement. Four days later my social worker called with an emergency placement. An eleven-year-old boy had been abandoned at a hospital, she said, and she needed a place for him to stay just for the weekend.

Two years later, Anthony was still with me. Not only did I finally allow him to call me Dad but we were also in the final stages of the adoption process so that I could be his dad forever. He was the first child I adopted. For Anthony, this was his second adoption. It was his adoptive parents who had abandoned him at the hospital. His bio parents abandoned him long before that. Because of his history, I had been very cautious about being apart from him for prolonged periods of time. Before I committed to speak at this conference in Seattle, I went over my schedule with him. The family with whom he was going to stay was close to us. Rather than present this as me going away, it was more about him having a great weekend with a terrific family.

But now Anthony was sick. I let out a long sigh and rubbed my head. From the sounds of it, he needed to see a doctor. I couldn't let someone else do that for me, not with Anthony's past. I think anyone who had been abandoned at a medical facility at age eleven would probably be triggered by going back to one.

"Okay," I said. "I'm going to head back to the airport and catch the next flight. Tell him I will be there as soon as I can."

I called the conference people and explained the situation. Since it was a conference on foster and adoptive kids, they of course understood. Then I called the airline and arranged my flight home. Finally, I checked out of the hotel room that I had barely touched and headed for the airport.

The flight back to North Carolina seemed so much longer than the flight out. I could not stop worrying about my son, though I thought he would be fine. Kids get sick all the time. But for a child who has lived through what my son has lived through, I hated the thought of him being so sick without me there. He'd had enough of that in his life.

It was quite late by the time I got to the sitter's house. They were waiting up for me. "How's Anthony?" I asked.

"About the same," she said. "He still can't hold anything down. He's exhausted from it."

"I can only imagine so," I said as I headed to the guest room to get him to take him home.

As soon as he saw me, Anthony smiled. Then his fever broke. He never threw up even once with me. Still, I took him to the hospital to get him checked out. Every test came back normal.

No fever.

No nausea.

No sickness at all.

The same thing happened the next time I went out of town. And the next. Anthony was not faking illness to get me to come home. The fever was real. The vomiting was real. The headache was real. He was a sick child . . . until he saw me. It was like a switch flipped, and he was miraculously healed.

The third time Anthony became ill while I was traveling without him, a light came on for me. Even though more than two years had passed since he had been abandoned, even though he felt very secure in my home, and even though I was his father just as surely as if he were my biological son for whom I had cared since the day of his birth, the roots of trauma from not one but two abandonments had not gone away. Today he is a strong, confident, well-adjusted young adult, and I could not be prouder of him. And yet, I know those roots still lurk below the surface because mine still do in me. While the wounds may heal and the scars fade, the roots of trauma never completely go away.

Today, as a fifty-year-old man, I recognize when my trauma is about to resurface along with the lies it tells me, like that I cannot trust anyone. That lie is always with me, but as an adult, I quiet it with truth. My son reacted to my leaving because he thought I was never coming back. That was the lie we had to work through together, as father and son.

No One Gets Through Life Unscathed

Foster and adoptive children are far from the only kids who experience trauma while growing up. We all go through very difficult times that leave their mark, and, as parents, we cannot prevent our children from being wounded. Trauma comes in many ways. For me, it was rejection. For others, it is abandonment. Divorce causes trauma for children, even when parents work to be as amicable as possible. A parent's, sibling's, or family member's addiction leaves an impact. The death of a parent, grandparent, or close relative inflicts trauma, as do all the events that get lumped together as "acts of God," like tornadoes, hurricanes, floods, and fires.

In other words, trauma takes on many forms and can impact us for a lifetime.

As one who started his life in a poor village in Africa, I saw traumatic events on a regular basis even before I ran away from home. Aside from being physically abused by my father, my worst experience came when I went to look for my little brother, who was late coming home from fetching water for the family. I found him face down in a puddle where he had fallen after he suffered an epileptic seizure. I still think about my brother and wonder why I didn't go fetch the water that day. In America, most of us are insulated from the bad parts of life, but they still happen. Even if we don't realize it, we don't just get over them. Yes, we grow and heal and can move past such events, but the trauma remains. James 1:2–4 tells us that God uses all our trials and suffering to shape our character and make us mature. Even so, no matter how much a traumatic event may help us grow stronger and more resilient, the roots of that trauma can still come up and cause problems or spark behavior that is difficult for us to understand.

When we have a child who has gone through trauma, the worst thing we can do is to tell them either verbally or through our actions that they just need to get over it. Instead, we need to validate their feelings and walk with them through their healing process. What's challenging is how very long and slow that process can be.

For me, I was probably twenty-five or twenty-six years old before I was finally able to receive an act of kindness from someone without immediately putting up my guard to protect myself from whatever they really planned to do to me. I cannot tell you how difficult it was for me to build and maintain friendships when I did not trust any other human being. I did not just get over those feelings. Instead, with time, I learned to recognize them, understand what they were, and manage them to prevent them from hindering my life going forward. Believe me, the roots are still there. To this day, my immediate reaction to the simplest act of kindness is to jump to the conclusion that this person is after something. I must consciously confront those feelings and manage them.

My own experience helps me to not lose patience when I see the roots of trauma bubbling up in my children's lives. I do my best to work with them and find ways to help them manage theirs as well. With Anthony, to help him get past becoming ill when I traveled, I prepared him weeks in advance for my trips. Then I sent him photos of me through every stage of my trip. We also used FaceTime to talk so that he could see I was exactly where I said I was going. And of course, I brought him home souvenirs from wherever I went. Even today there are times when, if he comes home from school and I'm not there, he will immediately call or text me with just a hint of panic, asking where I am. Once he knows, he's fine.

The fact that every human being faces some level of trauma does not diminish the fact that children in the foster care system have endured more than their fair share. Foster and adoptive parents face an even greater challenge because, for many of our children, the abnormal is normal for them. In other words, they lived in such chaos before coming into our homes that stability and normalcy feel overwhelmingly foreign. Our efforts to provide a safe, trauma-free environment can feel traumatic to them. When the lack of trauma feels traumatic to a child, they will often act out in a way that is way over the top to try to get themselves removed from our homes.

I once had a seven-year-old boy who had come from an abusive situation and had bounced around between several foster families. One morning I walked into my kitchen to discover him sitting on the kitchen island completely naked and doing things no seven-year-old should even know about. As soon as he saw me, his eyes locked on me, not with shock in being caught but more like he had been expecting me. My eyes nearly bugged out of my head, and I'm sure my jaw dropped.

Oh my gosh! What is happening here?!

No matter what thoughts ran through my head, I knew I could not react like I was shocked. So I took a breath and said, "Whenever you are finished with whatever you are doing, get dressed and we'll go out for breakfast."

Those were the last words he expected to hear come out of my mouth. Over breakfast he confided in me that he was certain I was going to send him back to the state's DCS (Department of Children's Services)[4] because other families had. He decided that if he was going to go out, he was going out with a bang. When I did not send him back and backed that up by continuing to love him, we were finally able to make progress with the abandonment and rejection issues that haunted him.

Trauma shapes a child. The effects of trauma never completely go away. Yet that is not the end of the story for a child. As parents, we can make a difference if we will stick with it when others want to give up. Part of loving children for who they are is understanding their stories and embracing them for who they are, scars and all.

---

4. Every state has a different name for the agency that runs their foster care system.

19

Rejection and Abandonment Make Accepting Love Nearly Impossible

I did not put on shoes for the first time until I was fifteen. In my home village, no one could afford to buy shoes for their children. Even if my family could have afforded them, my father never would have bought shoes for me. My mother worked very hard to make it possible for us to eat one meal every other day. If she had somehow found enough money to buy shoes for me and my siblings, she would have used it to buy enough food for us to eat every day. I would take food over shoes any day. Of course, when I ran away from home and lived on the streets of Kampala, no one ever gave me a pair of shoes. Not that I needed any. Even though I walked on hot pavement, over rocks, and even around broken glass, the calluses on the bottoms of my feet were so thick I never felt anything.

Calluses of the Heart

I made my heart the same way. I've already written about the verbal abuse my father threw at me on a daily basis. The more he told me he wished I'd never been born, the harder my heart became toward him so that his words could no longer hurt me. Every child naturally loves their parents. That's what made the verbal abuse even more painful than his physical abuse. I was my father's oldest son. I wanted him to love me and be proud of me, like every boy does. I envy those guys who say their dad is their best friend and their hero. I always wanted that from my own father. Instead he made it clear that I was garbage in his eyes. The calluses on my heart made his rejection hurt less and less until I could not feel it any longer. That was my way of winning. I wanted him to know that he could not hurt me even if he beat me to death.

My calluses only grew thicker and thicker after I ran away from home. I may have been hundreds of miles away from my father, but I could still feel the impact of his words. I made up my mind that no one was ever going to hurt me like that again. Life on the streets also demanded that I not let myself feel anything. I was just one of a group of boys who lived together next to a garbage dump and worked together to help us all survive. They were my friends, but we didn't let ourselves get too attached to one another. We might wake up one morning and find a friend had died in the night. It happened. If you let yourself get too close and feel too much, the odds increased that you'd be the next one dead. None of us even knew one another's real names or much of anything about anyone's life before they ended up on the streets. It was better that way. It was the only way to survive.

Many of our children who come into our homes through the foster care system are just like I was. They feel rejected and abandoned by their bio parents, especially those kids who have been in multiple foster homes. Our children love their bio parents, and yet they cannot understand why their mom or dad didn't do more to keep them together. Why did they let this happen to them? The longer a child is in the system, the greater their sense of rejection. The greater the sense of rejection, the thicker the calluses around their hearts and the less likely the child will let you get close enough to love them like a mom or a dad. They've already had Mom or Dad or both reject them. There's no way they are going to give you the chance to hurt them in the same way.

I know all this is true because I have lived on the other side. When James befriended me, I was just a stranger living on the streets. He paid my way to attend a boarding school where I not only received an education but also had three meals a day along with a safe place to live. During school breaks, James and his family had me stay with them. They told me I was a part of their family and treated me like a son. James and his wife showed me genuine love and kindness. Still, I never let them in. Letting them get close enough to hurt me made about as much sense to me as scraping the calluses off my feet when I did not have shoes. All I could possibly accomplish was to open myself up to a great deal of pain. I'd had enough pain from my bio father. I wasn't going to let these strangers hurt me too. I didn't even have to make a conscious choice to shut them out. The calluses were already there. At the time, I was incapable of receiving love from anyone.

As foster parents, we have children with such deep calluses that they, too, are incapable of receiving love from us. They developed their calluses to protect themselves from more emotional pain. There's no way they are opening themselves up to a stranger, and that's what we are. They don't just get over the pain of rejection from their parents and other adults who were supposed to love them. My oldest son, Anthony, went through this with both his bio and his first adoptive parents. He may have asked if he could call me Dad the first day he was with me, but that didn't mean he was ready to be vulnerable with me or any adult.

It is easy to become frustrated with our kids when they do not respond to us or ever seem to accept us as their parents. With foster children who may only be in our homes for a few weeks or months, we don't expect them to fully open up to us. However, when we adopt, we do expect our love to be reciprocated. We've taken the ultimate step to show our kids our love is real, that we truly are their forever family who only wants their best for them. Our kids even believe this themselves, but dropping their guard and opening themselves fully to us may never come, even though they now share our name. Like I wrote in an earlier chapter, this is what we signed up for.

So How Do I Love a Child Who Struggles to Accept My Love?

I know I drove James and his wife crazy with how I kept them at arm's length for years. I never yelled at them or used the line I've heard as a foster dad a million times: "You aren't my parents!" Instead, I tried to be the perfect child. After every meal I jumped up and started clearing dishes. I kept my room spotless. I helped around the house, doing anything I saw that needed to be done without asking. I took school incredibly seriously and worked to have top grades in every class. In the process I alienated James's bio children. It was like I was going out of my way to make them look bad. Of course, I wasn't. I was only trying to repay every kindness the family had shown me so that I was not in their debt. My experience told me that eventually that debt would have to be repaid, and I was determined to do it on my terms. Of course, I was completely wrong. Nothing had to be repaid. James and his wife did not expect anything back from me any more than they expected their bio kids to repay them for doing basic parenting stuff. It took a long time, but I slowly but surely started to open myself up and accept my foster parents' love. Thankfully, they were patient with me and let me come around on my terms, not theirs.

I take this same approach with my children, whether they are only with me a few months or become part of my forever family through adoption. We cannot scrape away a child's calluses and force them to become vulnerable. Doing so feels like an act of violence. No one responds positively to violence. I know none of us ever thinks that we are trying to force our will on our children. However, to them it feels that way, especially if we force them to do even small things, like calling us Mom and Dad before they are ready, if they ever are. We cannot force love. We can only demonstrate it and be willing to let it go unreciprocated. The process is long, but when we see the payoff, it is worth it.

I have a son who came to me while in high school. When he first came, I offered to get him a phone and put him on my phone plan. "No, I don't need a phone," he replied. I could see myself saying the same thing to my foster parents when I was his age (except we didn't have cell phones!).

"Everyone your age needs a phone," I said. The phone was as much for me to call and text him as it was for him.

"If I want one, I will pay for it myself," he said.

I explained how the state gave me money to put toward his phone, but he was adamant. He did not want me to give him a phone. He said the same thing when I offered to take him shopping to get him new clothes. "I have all the clothes I need," he said. Again, I told him that the state gave me money just to buy him clothes, but he still said no. "When I need some, I will buy them."

He never explained why, but I knew. He was just like me when I lived with James and his family. His walls were up, and he wasn't going to open the door for something as small as a phone or some clothes.

Over the next couple of years he softened a little, but he still had trouble opening up. For foster and adoptive kids, accepting our love often feels like they are betraying their bio parents. My son's bio father had never been a part of his life, and his mother had moved across the country after he was removed from her home, but he remained loyal to them. I didn't press him on it; I just stayed consistent in my love for him.

My son's story is long, and it is his to tell, but I finally got to see a breakthrough. He aged out of the system and even left my house to go off in search of both his mom and his dad when he turned eighteen, like nearly all foster children do. However, we stayed in touch. He came back to my home for visits and eventually finished high school. My family and I of course went to be a part of his big day. At one point in the middle of the celebration, he was talking to his bio mom and turned to ask me a question. He started his question with a word that is music to my ears.

He called me Dad.

He had called me Dad before. He always called me Dad when he was in my home. But we weren't in my home. We were with his biological mother—his "real" parent. Yet he still called me Dad because that's what I had finally become to him. The calluses were gone. I was his father, and he was my son even though I'd never formally adopted him.

Here's the beautiful part of this story: for me, the moment would have been just as sweet if he'd called me Peter. He didn't have to call me Dad for me to love him as his father, and he knew that. Because that's what parents do: we simply love. And it's how we handle loving a child who struggles to accept it. We just love no matter how the story may end.

20

You Can't Trust Your Kids and They Don't Trust You. Now What?

The greatest difference between bio children and foster or adopted children is this: your bio children instinctively trust you. From the moment they are born, you are the constant in their lives. When they are hungry, you feed them. When they are upset, you soothe them. When they are tired, you hold them and rock them to sleep. When they wake up, you are there. You are the one thing they know they can depend on, even when they are too young to express this as conscious thought. Your baby wants you, needs you, loves you, and trusts you above anyone else on the planet.

Kids in foster care have had this trust ripped away. By the time they get to us, they've been shuffled around between so many relatives and so many foster homes and group homes and more foster homes. We may be foster home number twelve. Any sense of trust they have is long gone. Even if we are foster home number one, and they come straight to our homes from their bio parents, the one constant in their lives is now gone and their instinctive trust has been broken. No one should honestly believe these kids will come into our homes and instantly transfer that trust onto us. We are all starting from scratch with our foster and adopted children. We have to earn that trust.

But that's not the only difference between bio children and those who come into our homes through foster care or adoption.

When your baby begins to grow and moves from infant to toddler to young child, you are the greatest influence in their life. You teach them and shape them. Because you know your child, you trust them. Of course they do things they should not do. That is human nature. But you correct them and teach them right from wrong. Young children want to please their parents, which means that even as they test your rules and boundaries, most of the time they will try to do what is right in your eyes. The whole relationship is built on trust. Our biggest challenges as parents come when our children break that trust, as eventually they all do to some degree. However, even when a child breaks our trust, we can draw upon that common experience of them growing up in our home since birth to try to rebuild it.

Blind trust with a foster or adopted child is a recipe for disaster. A kid who is already drinking at age eleven isn't going to stop trying to get alcohol any way they can just because they now live in your home. A kid who started smoking weed before age twelve is not going to lose their desire to smoke just because they come into a home that does not allow it. A kid who steals is going to keep on stealing. A kid who lies is going to keep on lying. A kid who grew up watching porn because it was always on in their home or even played out live in front of them is not going to suddenly think porn is something no child should ever see. Does this mean that every child who comes into our homes is a dope-smoking alcoholic compulsive liar and thief with a pornography addiction? Of course not! But if we assume they are angels who would never lie to us or steal or drink or touch drugs or watch inappropriate shows and movies, we are only fooling ourselves and setting both ourselves and our children up for failure. I've never had bio children, but I think the same holds true for them. If I blindly trust my children and assume they will never do any of the things I tell them not to do, I am in trouble as a dad.

The fact that our foster and adoptive children do not trust us when they come into our homes only makes the situation harder. Every home has rules and boundaries, including mine. But in addition to the house rules, I also set up guardrails to protect my kids from themselves. The house computer is one example. All my kids have access to it, but I have installed tracking software and given each child their own individual settings. I also installed a camera in the computer room so that I can see and track who is on the computer at any given time and see exactly what they are doing. Of course, if all my children had been born into my family, I would do the same thing. There's too much bad on the internet to simply turn my children loose to discover it on their own. I also installed the same sort of software on all the devices in our house: phones, iPads, tablets. If it can access the internet, I put something on it to both protect and track my kids.

When a child who has never had anyone even care what they do online comes into my home, they see my rules and guardrails as something like prison bars. They don't just complain and tell me how unfair I am or how much they hate it in my home; they start plotting a prison break. Smart kids will find their way around the safety software, and when I confront them, they deny everything. They don't just deny they've done anything wrong; they turn it around and call me a liar, just like every other foster parent they have met. It doesn't matter that I have the tracking software and camera footage that clearly shows them doing exactly what they deny doing. In their eyes, I am the liar and I am the bad guy.

The same happens with all my rules and boundaries. I've had to remove doors from kids' rooms because they repeatedly did things behind their closed doors that they knew they should not do. Removing their door makes a child almost as happy as blocking their access to sites they shouldn't visit or turning off the internet completely at 11:00 p.m. Some days I am very popular with my kids (sarcasm intended).

Those are the days I often find myself sitting outside in my car, trying to push myself to go inside because I know what is waiting for me on the other side. It can feel like a no-win situation.

This, then, is the dilemma we face: How can we earn our children's trust while also learning to trust them?

Earning and Learning

One of the hardest things we will ever do as foster and adoptive parents is convince our children that we have their best interests at heart at all times. Children in foster care don't believe anyone but themselves have their best interests at heart. Adults don't, at least not the adults who were supposed to care for them in the past. Those relationships have often proven disappointing and unreliable. The people they counted on the most let them down the hardest. And now we come along and say, "You can trust me. I want what is best for you. I want to help you succeed in life." Even if the child wants to believe you, beneath the surface is the fear that they cannot count on you because eventually you are going to leave them just like everyone else. For them, the first step toward earning trust is simply getting the child to believe you are not going to abandon them.

Because many of our children have experienced rejection and abandonment, they have extreme separation anxiety, which is a form of mistrust. That is, we say we are only going to the bathroom, but experience tells them not to believe we will come back. One trust-building exercise I learned from Marissa Bradford is to tell the child, "I have to go to the bathroom now, and it is something I prefer to do alone. I will be out of the bathroom in five minutes." You then proceed to the bathroom, close and lock the door, and stay in there for exactly five minutes. The child may yell and scream and pound on the door, or, even scarier, may be completely silent and give you no idea of what they are doing. However they respond, after exactly five minutes, you exit the bathroom and connect with the child. If they are screaming or crying, you comfort them. If they shun you, you talk to them about your absence and how you did exactly what you said you were going to do. Repeat the same procedure every time you go to the bathroom as well as any other time you have to be apart from them for a set amount of time. Over time, as you always show back up, the child will begin to believe that when you say you will be back, you will keep your promise. That's the first step of trust.

Trust also comes as we provide a structured home environment, with clear and developmentally appropriate boundaries. Setting boundaries is easy. Staying consistent with them and with the consequences for crossing them is much harder. But it is the consistency that teaches children they can trust you. Children who come from hard places where there were no rules or consequences or any kind of stability will at first find such structure to be like living in a different world. At times this world can be overwhelming to them. I've had kids who responded by trying to break as many of the rules in my house as possible or doing something dramatic to try to get themselves removed from my home, like the boy I found sitting naked on the kitchen counter one morning I wrote about earlier. If we respond to the behavior with compassion and dignity, we go a long way toward earning their trust. If we react . . . it may be game over.

Believe it or not, one of the signs that our children are starting to trust us can come through them breaking our rules. Over time, as they sense we are trustworthy, they may feel like we can handle the truth about who they are and what they do. They may stop trying to hide their smoking or drinking to see how we will deal with it. This is also a way for them to test how committed we are to what we say about having their best interests at heart. Instead of sneaking around, they may pull out a joint right in front of us to see how we are going to react. At this point, parents can address the behaviors with the same consistency used in gaining the child's initial trust, prioritizing love and predictable consequences. In other words, we can actually begin to trust them.

I know that last sounds counterintuitive. Yet I have found that when they stop trying to hide bad behavior, I no longer have to act like a detective trying to solve a crime. I now know exactly what I am dealing with because it is right in front of me. No more secrets. No more lies. At this stage it may feel like the only thing we can trust this kid to do is exactly what we don't want them to do. However, even this stage gives us a foundation on which we can begin to build a real relationship. It opens the door to talk about why they want to do these things and get down to the root behind the behavior.

Thankfully, most of the time we will not find ourselves in the most extreme situations. With most of our kids, as they begin to trust us, their behavior changes for the better. As it does, we are able to trust them and relax some of the boundaries. I still have to watch out when we go to someone else's home or they have a babysitter while I go out. One of my biggest rules is no sugary drinks after 4:00 in the afternoon. I cannot tell you how many times I've come back to find my kids wired on sugar because they convinced the sitter otherwise. Tricking a sitter I can handle, and I almost expect it because it's pretty much normal kid behavior. The best days are when one of my kids tries to trick the sitter but another child speaks up and says, "No, Dad didn't say that." These moments will come. Like every other part of being a foster or adoptive parent, we just have to be consistent and patient.

One Final Dose of Reality

I know that last paragraph sounds so encouraging, but also keep in mind that our kids figure out the system pretty quickly—and know how to use it to try to get what they want. The biggest tool they have in their pocket to try to manipulate us or to get removed from our home is to tell the social worker that we have hit them or abused them in some way. Of course it is a lie, but it works. As soon as the child utters the word *abuse*, they are immediately removed from your home, as well as every other child in your home. I have had this happen to me twice. A child comes into my home and doesn't want to be there. The only place they want to be is back home with Mom and Dad. They know that when they said something to a teacher about the abuse they were enduring at home, the social workers came and removed them from the home. In their little mind, they now think that if they accuse me of abuse, the social workers will come, take them from my home, and send them back to Mom and Dad's house. Of course it doesn't happen that way.

Instead, I've endured two months of investigations by DCS to prove what they suspected from the start: the child had lied to try to work the system to get what they wanted. I felt like I was in jail or under house arrest while they cleared my name. Believe me when I say that it becomes harder to trust the children who come into my home after going through this once, much less twice! I have friends who have quit as foster parents after they went through this sort of false accusation. I don't blame them, but I cannot join them. Parenting without trust is a challenge that does not end. The best we can do is hang on to the small victories when we do break through with a child.

21

For Children from Hard Places, Abnormal Is Normal

Nearly every child seems nervous when they walk into a new foster home for the first time. My other kids, especially my adopted kids, help make my house feel inviting, but a new foster child still has their guard up. They look around, wide-eyed, taking everything in like they are trying to figure this place out. Most barely talk when I introduce myself because they are trying to figure me out as well. I do my best to make them feel at home as quickly as possible, but it still takes them a while to get even semi-comfortable.

When six-year-old Jacob came through my door with a social worker, he wasn't just nervous. He was on edge like he was just waiting for something bad to happen. "Hi Jacob, I'm Peter," I said with a warm smile. He didn't reply. Instead he gave me a look that made me think I was looking at an eighteen-year-old, not a six-year-old little boy. He didn't show fear. Instead, his look basically said, *What is wrong with you?* That was a new one for me from a child this young.

I showed him his room and where to put his things. He just sort of nodded to acknowledge me. "Okay then, I will let you get settled in," I said. "I will be in the living room. Let me know if you need anything." He sort of gave me a nod and a grunt. As I was about to leave the room he finally spoke and said, "Yo, b–h, go get me some water."

Wait. What? Did this six-year-old boy just say what I thought he said?

"Excuse me," I said. "What did you say?"

"I said b–h go get me some water."

I went over to him and got down on one knee so that we were at eye level. "Jacob, here in this house, we do not use that kind of language." He actually smirked at me. Again, he was six. "I know where you came from that may have been how everyone talked. But not here. We do not call people names like that," I said. "Do you understand?"

Jacob gave me the once-over, like he was trying to figure out what kind of weak-kneed wimp I had to be. "It's how my mom's boyfriend talks to her," he said with attitude.

"I understand," I said, "but we do not speak to one another in that way in this house. Everyone is treated with respect."

In my mind I was simply telling Jacob to be kind to me and to everyone in my family. However, the look he gave me made it clear that in his mind I was now insulting his mother and her boyfriend. I was essentially telling him that his mother was wrong and that the way they did things in his bio home was not just wrong but completely unacceptable.

If he had his doubts about me before, Jacob now made up his mind that he could not trust me, that he did not need to listen to me, and that I was a fool and a threat—and there was nothing I could do to change it. All of this happened within the first ten minutes of him coming into my home simply by my asking him to speak like a normal six-year-old when, in his mind, he already was. "Normal," for a child, is the behavior modeled by their parents. When many of those same behaviors are the very things that cause a child to be removed from a home, foster parents must be prepared for just about anything.

The Easy Part

A child's abnormal normal can be just about anything, from language, to too-mature television shows and movies, to inappropriate touching, all the way down to something as small as a stinky blanket. I've dealt with them all, but I must admit the blanket was a new one for me. Lots of children have security blankets. Over the years, I've seen many blankets come out of the black garbage bag social workers throw a child's possessions into to go with them to a new home. But one blanket stands out in my memory, not because of how it looked but because of its smell. It smelled disgusting, almost like it was something pulled out of a garbage dump. And it was *so* dirty. I don't know that it had ever been washed. Honestly, I thought it might be a health risk to the child. It looked like it was crawling with diseases.

When the child pulled the blanket out for the first time, my first reaction was to say, "Hey, buddy, do you want me to wash that for you?"

I might as well have asked if I could set it on fire. He not only cried but also tightened his grip on the blanket so hard that I knew I'd never pry his fingers off it.

"Okay, that's all right," I said, trying to calm him down. "No one is going to do anything with your blanket."

Inside, my mind was racing, trying to think of some way to wash that nasty thing. But as it turns out, I never washed the blanket. It wasn't just that this child thought dirty and stinky was normal. Whenever the child became upset, he pulled the blanket up close to his face and breathed in the stench. When I asked him why, he told me it smelled like home. Sure, I could have insisted on washing the blanket because it was making my entire house stink, and once it came out of the dryer, it would smell fresh and clean. But to do so would mean robbing this small child of his one constant reminder of the home he left behind. My home smelled clean (or at least as clean as I could keep it with a houseful of children), but clean felt foreign to my child. His stinky blanket was normal to him, and that brought him comfort. I wasn't about to take that away from him.

I also have children come to me who have never had a fresh, home-cooked meal. Normal food for them comes from a box.

Cookies from a box.

Mac and cheese from a box.

Crackers from a box.

Box. Box. Box.

For them, normal food is not cooked on a stove. Normal meals are microwaved. When I use pots and pans, they are almost like, *Whoa, what are those?!* Any meals they eat that don't come from a box come from a fast-food restaurant. And their favorites are always fried. Normal food swims up to your plate from a pool of oil. Then you drown it in ketchup. Normal food also comes only in shades of brown, unless it is in the candy or sweet cereal food group. If I put out a dish of green vegetables, they look at it like I dropped a snake on the table. Fresh fruit is more of the same. Fruits are flavors of Gatorade or Mountain Dew. And of course there are the universal American staples of bacon and chocolate. Most of my kids don't know what to do with a peach or an apple, but they love bacon and chocolate.

Do we want our children to live on box meals, chicken nuggets, and chocolate-covered bacon? Of course not. That should never be considered a normal diet. However, we cannot force our children to suddenly change their eating habits, not if we want to build a relationship with them. What we can do is mix in some of our children's favorites from their bio homes. It doesn't matter if we find oil-soaked fried "chicken" nuggets smothered in ketchup to be disgusting. For our kids, it gives them a happy reminder of their life before, even for those who have very few happy memories.

When we can incorporate our children's "abnormal" foods, clothes, or even a stinky blanket into their new normal routine in our homes, we go a long way toward establishing trust with them. The same holds for the traditions and elements of our children's cultures that are very different from ours. Even when we adopt our children, we are not asking them to forget their pasts. Instead, we need to find ways to celebrate that which was good. If that means including some strange food in our Thanksgiving or Christmas celebrations that does not fit into our normal, so be it. Including it communicates love and acceptance for every part of our children, including who they were before they ever met us.

And Now It Gets More Difficult

Some things, however, are simply not acceptable. Remember, what is normal to a child is whatever was modeled consistently in their home from the time they were born. For our kids, many have parents who have shown them that getting drunk and getting high are completely normal. These kids watched their bio parents do drugs and drink heavily in front of them. Some even have parents who had the children join them. They also have parents who watched the absolute worst things imaginable right in front of them. Sex. Extreme violence. The worst

R-rated movies ever made and even pornography are what some of my kids as young as four and five have thought of as normal shows to watch, not *Bluey* or *Daniel Tiger*. Even worse, actual sex and violence in the home have also been normal parts of everyday life. Some of my kids have watched as a husband or boyfriend beat up their mother. Some have witnessed drugs being dealt right in front of them as well as various sex acts as payment. Some of these kids have seen worse than the worst we can imagine, not just once but over and over until it was a completely normal part of their lives. No one protected them or tried to preserve their innocence as children. They've not only seen the worst but the worst is normal.

And then they are removed from those homes and come into ours. When it is time to pick out a show, one will say, "I want to watch . . ." and they name some incredibly graphic violent movie with extended sex scenes. This comes from small children. "No," we tell them, "that movie is not appropriate for children to watch."

"But I watched it with my mom!"

This isn't a dirty blanket. And it isn't chocolate-covered bacon. No five-year-old needs to watch *Pulp Fiction* to remind them of watching movies with their mother. Not that a five-year-old understands this. What we are basically telling the child is that what their mother or father let them watch and do was wrong. One of the saddest parts of fostering is working with children who had their innocence robbed from them. We are now tasked with resetting boundaries in part to restore their innocence. While we can never take away what they have been exposed to thus far in their young lives, we can stop the damage from spreading further by stopping any future exposure.

It isn't easy. When one of our kids first opens up about what they have seen and experienced, our first reaction is one of shock and judgment. I get mad. I can't help it. But getting angry doesn't help our children. We see the things to which our children have been exposed as dangerous. And they are. I've had teens whom I discovered were dealing drugs at school. To me, that's a ticket to prison. For them, it's the family business. They grew up watching drug deals go down from the time they were in a high chair. Our getting mad over their past doesn't help them in the present.

Instead of becoming angry and judging them and their parents, we need to listen first. Judgment often creates feelings of shame in our kids, an emotion that children who are in foster care already experience more frequently and more deeply than most. When our kids open up to us about an experience or idea from their bio homes, we need to show interest and appreciation. That is, appreciation for them feeling safe enough to share with us. Some thoughts that children share are chaotic, weird, concerning, and disturbing. Even still, suspending expressions of judgment keeps the door to conversation and understanding open for foster parents.

The next step is setting boundaries along with age-appropriate consequences. "Age-appropriate" is a bit tricky with foster kids because, although these kids have seen stuff far beyond their age, emotionally and developmentally many lag behind where they should be. I've found that many times a ten-year-old is developmentally closer to a seven-year-old while trying to do stuff they can't legally do until they are twenty-one. The consequences we set need to fit their level of understanding.

Trying to undo the hold of an abnormal sense of normalcy is not a short-term project. Nor is it something we have to attempt on our own. Speaking only for myself, even understanding all of this on the most basic level can feel overwhelming. This is an area in which I depend on counselors and therapists to help my children. I have also had instances where even that was not enough. You may have reached this point as well. It is okay to say that you've come to a place that is more than you can handle. Sometimes, the damage inflicted before our kids ever arrive in our homes is so severe that they may need to be admitted to a care facility that can give them the help they need. Doing so is not giving up on a child. Instead it is an ultimate act of love that says, like every other part of parenting should, "More than anything, I want what is best for my child and their long-term future." Some might say that doesn't feel normal for a parent. Of course it doesn't, but nothing about the foster parent experience fits anyone's definition of normal.

22

Your Children Are Torn Between Two Worlds

I love my father.

Yes, I ran away from home at the age of ten to escape his abuse.

And yes, I still love him.

When I was sixteen and doing well as a student at my boarding school, I did odd jobs to raise enough money to travel back to my home village. I wanted to see my mother but also to let my father know that he could never hurt me again. In my home village, only the wealthiest people owned shoes. So I went back with two pairs of shoes, just to rub my new standing in my father's face. More than anything I wanted him to know that I had already done more with my life at age sixteen than he would ever do with his. In that visit, he received that message loud and clear. He avoided contact with me the best he could while I was home, which in our culture was a sign of embarrassment.

I also stood up to him in a way no one had before. One night I heard my father yelling at my mother just outside their house. Immediately, I went outside and jumped between him and my mom. I told him never to speak to her like that again.

"Do you think you can stop me?" he asked.

"Bring it, old man," I replied. "I am not afraid of you, and I will stop you."

Just like that, my father backed down and walked away in shame. I loved every second of his humiliation, yet, deep down, it made me sad. I didn't want to have to protect my mother from him. I wanted him to love my mother, to love me, and to treat my brothers and sisters with respect. But for him, that was impossible. After I stood up to him, he spent the rest of the night in the local bar getting drunk.

All my life I've wanted a genuine relationship with my father, but even at age ten, when I ran away, I knew the relationship I instinctively longed for was never going to happen. Now, more than four decades later, nothing has changed. I speak to my mom over the phone at least once a week, but I never talk to my dad. When I go back to my home village, I spend lots of time with my mom and other relatives. My dad spends as little time around me as possible. I'm okay with that. I don't expect anything more from him because I know who and what he is.

And even so, he's my father, and I love him.

I chose to escape my father's abuse, yet I still feel the longing in my heart for a real relationship with him. In a sense, I am torn between the longing every child has for the love of their parents and the reality of how life really is. If I feel this pull some forty years after choosing to get away from this abusive man, imagine how conflicted our children feel. The vast majority did not choose to leave their bio parents. The state made that decision for them. If it were up to our kids, most would say they never wanted to be separated from their parents. Even those who know they needed to be removed for their own safety hope to go back someday. They are literally torn between the home and life they have with us and their longing to be back with their parents, even if the latter is a much worse living situation.

Our kids know it, but most don't care.

They love their parents and want to be with them no matter what.

We Are Competing with a Fantasy World

I do not mean to downplay what our children went through in their bio homes that caused them to be removed. When our children are with us long enough and we earn a level of their trust, some will open up and tell us a little of what they have experienced. A lot of it we can guess by our kids' behavior without having to be told. But when the stories come, they are hard to hear. I constantly tell myself to listen and not react. The last thing I want to do is get angry and have my child stop sharing or get mad at me for being mad at their mom or dad.

Yet I find it difficult to control my anger when a child tells me a horrible story about their mom having sex with different men for drug money right in front of them at one moment, then turns around and talks about how wonderful life is going to be when they go back home. "And she's working really hard to get me back," they nearly always say. It's like our kids have retreated inside a fantasy world. If we try to blow it up and bring them back to reality, we risk alienating them forever. I hate this part of being a foster dad.

I can understand how my kids build this fantasy world. It begins with a wish. My kids miss their parents so much that they believe their parents must miss them just as much. My kids will do anything to be reunited, and they project that belief onto their parents.

"Did you know my mom has stopped using drugs?" my child will tell me.

"Really?" I'll say.

"She promised me she was going to so that I can go home. I know she's going to quit for me."

My heart always sinks during these conversations. I do not doubt that my child's mom meant it when she made this promise. I also have no doubt that the mom loves this child and would do anything within her power to get them back. But as an adult, I also know the power of addiction and how that pull can keep even the most loving, well-meaning of parents away from their kids.

Supervised visitation times with the bio parents only feed a child's fantasies of home and take them to a new level. Part of me hates visitation days. It's not that I want to keep my kids away from their bio parents. Reunification is the goal of foster care, and, for my children's sake, I want to see that happen. I hate visitation times because of what they do to my kids.

It starts days before the actual visit. My child's anxiety increases, and their behavior goes downhill, all in anticipation of hopefully seeing their parents. *Hopefully* is the key word because, much of the time, the bio parents do not show up. Then it is up to me to pick up the pieces for my distraught child. I hate it. My kids hate it. And yet they cannot wait for the next visitation time.

Even when the two-hour supervised visitation time goes well, it is a poor measure of a parent's progress toward getting the child back while giving the child completely unrealistic expectations of both how soon they will get to go home and what life will be like when they return. When the parents show up, they bring sweet sodas, candy, and treats. At my house I limit how much of these my kids can have, but on a visitation time with Mom and Dad, they get as much as they want. My kids also get to do nothing but have fun with their bio parents, whether it is going to a park or playing video games. There's no homework, no chores, no following rules. They don't do anything like real life. The parents only get these visits once a week, so they want to make them special for their kids.

Beyond the sweets and games, the biggest difference between a supervised visit and life in the bio parents' home is what the children do *not* have to endure. No one is fighting and arguing during supervised visits. No one is getting drunk or high. No one is selling drugs. No one is doing any of the things that caused the children to be removed from the home in the first place. In a six-year-old's mind, that means their parents aren't doing those things anymore at home, either. They're doing better. They've changed. And because of that, our kids think they're going to get to go home soon.

But they don't get to go home soon.

The average child in foster care spends twenty-two months in the system. When they get out of the system, only 46 percent are reunited with their bio parents. Twenty-seven percent are adopted, usually by the foster parents, while another 11 percent go into guardianship or kinship placements.[5] An eight-year-old child doesn't understand any of this. From their perspective, everything has changed. There is no reason they can't go back home. Unfortunately, we, the foster parents, know better.

When one of my little ones comes back from a supervised visit smelling like weed, I know the bio mom is no closer to

5. Nicole Davi, "Foster Care and Adoption Statistics—AFCARS Annual Update," National Council for Adoption, March 20, 2024, https://adoptioncouncil .org/article/foster-care-and-adoption-statistics/.

getting her daughter back than when the child was removed from her home two years earlier. Of course, I can't be the one to break this news to my child. Our children aren't the only ones torn between these two worlds. We are too. If we tear down our children's fantasies of home, our kids see it as an attack on the people they love the most. Even when they love us (and they often do reciprocate our love), when push comes to shove, they will side with their bio parents over us almost every time. We cannot be the ones to destroy a child's fantasies of what they hope life will be like when they finally get to be with their parents again. Instead, our job is to provide healing for the past that can prepare our children to deal with whatever the future will hold regarding Mom and Dad.

Guarding Our Own Hearts

When we see all that bio parents continue to put our children through, on top of the trauma our children have already suffered, we naturally want to protect our kids. The urge to protect can slide into a mindset of us against them where the bio parents are the bad guys, the enemy. They put our kids through hell. They inflicted more trauma than any child should have to endure. They are the ones who rarely make it to their visits, and when they do they are stoned out of their minds. They, the bio parents, are the problem.

Since the bio parents are the problem, it is easy to see ourselves as the solution. The saviors. Not only are we going to protect these children but we are going to rescue them by creating a life for them that they are never going to want to leave. The bio parents will have no one to blame but themselves. They had their chance, but they blew it. We're going to pick up the pieces and fix the lives they broke.

Let me make one thing very, very clear: taking on a savior mentality will do far more harm than good to the children. If this is your mindset going into foster care, don't do it. Don't. I know these kids need homes, but they need homes that will prepare them to be reunited with the bio family they left behind. A savior mentality where the parents are the enemy is also toxic to any relationship you hope to have with a child. If we are to truly love the child, then we must love who they love. And they love their parents. So must we.

Parents who have their children removed by the state and placed into foster care deserve and need our compassion, not our judgment. Many of the parents who have their children placed in the foster care system were themselves foster kids. Statistics show that 70 percent of all girls who go through foster care are pregnant before they turn twenty-one. Seventy percent! That small child who comes into our homes may well indeed be the child of a mom who was in the same system just a few years earlier. It is a vicious cycle that can only be broken by our helping the mom gain the skills to be a good mother as much as helping the child heal from their past.

When people criticize parents who have their children removed from their homes, it feels very, very personal to me. In my first book, *Now I Am Known*, I talked a lot about how no one cared if one of us street kids got run over by the bus we happened to be sleeping under. We had no value. One less street kid meant one less kid bugging people by begging for money.

That was my side of the story.

My mother also felt the same scorn. Early on, after running away from home, I sent word with someone traveling to my home village to tell my mother that I was alive. I did not want her to worry about me. However, my mother was not the only one in my village who was told about me living on the streets.

The whole village heard the news, and they looked down on my mother because of it. People whispered about her and insulted her to her face. She became that woman whose son was human trash. Her son was a beggar. A thief. And worse.

My mother wore that shame until I returned home to her at age sixteen. When my village saw my clothes and my two pairs of shoes, and when they heard how I was getting an education, my mother went from reviled to revered. Then, when I not only went on to graduate from college but also sent money back home so that my siblings could all be educated, my mom became an honored member of the village. Yet I never forgot the stories of what people said about her when I was on the streets. She didn't deserve that, and neither do the bio parents of our children.

Again, if we love our kids, we will love those whom they love. And we do not have much time to wait to start. The harsh reality of being a foster parent is that our primary goal is to one day say goodbye and send our children home, whether we like it or not.

23

You Have to Be Prepared to Say Goodbye

The hardest part of my first placement with Kaine wasn't what you might expect.

It was not him slamming his head through a window.

It also was not him running away from me and screaming his way through a Chuck E. Cheese until someone called the police.

It wasn't even the calls from the school asking me to come back because he had flipped over a table or hit another child.

No, the hardest part of having Kaine in my life came eight months after he arrived, when I had to tell him goodbye. I cried. Kaine cried. His mother cried. We all cried together until Kaine, his mother, and the social worker walked out to a car to drive Kaine to an aunt's house, where he was to live permanently. It was one of the hardest days of my life up to that point. I've had many more since.

Telling a child goodbye who has been in my care for six, eight, or twelve months, or even longer, is never easy. Yet, when we sign up to become foster parents, we also sign up for the goodbyes. Reunification is always the goal, from the family courts to the social workers to the parents and the children. By definition, a foster care placement is supposed to be temporary. When Kaine first came to my house, I thought his stay might be very, very temporary. He would go from calmly sitting on a chair to spinning around and around on the floor, arms out, crashing into walls, screaming and crying at the top of his lungs in no time flat. Just as quickly, he'd stop and go back to being that calm child like he'd flipped a switch. Of course, in the beginning the switch flipped back to calm only after I bribed him with my iPad or phone.

With time, I began to understand what set Kaine off and how to help him regain control of himself without resorting to bribery. Over the months, the calls from the school became fewer and fewer until I rarely heard from them. I watched Kaine make so much progress, and through it, the two of us bonded. He called me Dad, I called him Son, and we both genuinely meant what we said. However, I knew from the time that the social worker first called about placing him with me that adoption was not going to be an option. Kaine was Native American, and under state law in Oklahoma, where I lived at the time, only a Native American family could adopt a Native American child. The law is designed to protect their heritage and culture. I understood the law, and I agreed whole-heartedly with it . . . until the time came to start getting Kaine ready to leave my home. I didn't want him to leave. He didn't want to leave. But it was not our decision to make. While his mother was not able to regain custody, an aunt had stepped up to raise him.

Thankfully, the courts didn't rule that Kaine was to be re-moved from me and placed with his aunt without warning. I did not want that, and his aunt certainly did not want that. She knew all about Kaine's behavioral issues from before he was removed from his mother's home. While she had agreed to take him, she wasn't completely sure she could handle him long-term. The two of us, along with Kaine's mother, worked together to prepare her for Kaine. Thankfully, Kaine was going to be the only child in her home, which was a relief to me. He would need her undivided attention. The aunt was also willing to learn everything I had learned about Kaine, from how to spot the warning signs of a meltdown to how to prepare him in advance for any change in routine. By the time he went to live with her, she knew all his favorite foods, shows, and routines, as well as all the things to avoid.

Two months before the transition, Kaine and I started going to his aunt's home for visits, which eventually turned into overnight stays. Then came the day I had to say goodbye. I thought I was prepared. I thought the transition phase would make it easier for me to see him go. I even told his aunt she could call me anytime, day or night, whenever she needed me.

And then he was gone.

Even though I had a couple of other children in my home, I felt very alone. Part of my heart left with Kaine, and it remains with him to this day. Thankfully, I have been able to keep in contact with him and his aunt. At first, she called because she needed answers ASAP during one of Kaine's meltdowns. With time, she called simply because he missed me and wanted to talk to me. Eventually, I suspect he may forget all about me. He was young when he left. He has many other people in his life and new memories that, with time, will make his eight months with me feel like a dream he sort of remembers.

But isn't that exactly what our role as a foster parent is supposed to be?

Our Worst Fears

I have found that the two biggest issues that keep people from becoming foster parents or cause them to give up after their first placement are: (1) they do not know how they can possibly let a child go, and (2) they do not believe they can deal with a child's trauma. In other words, the possibility of having to say goodbye to a child in whom they have invested their hearts and lives is more of a barrier than any other part of the foster parent experience. Believe me, I get this! I have fostered over forty children, and aside from the three I adopted, I have had to say goodbye to them all. Obviously, the bonds we build with our children make even thinking about letting them go extremely difficult. When a child is in our home, that child becomes *our* child. We truly become Mom or Dad. Of course, some children never let us make that connection. They keep their walls up the entire time they are in our home. Believe it or not, I have found those are some of the hardest to watch leave when it is time to say goodbye.

However, the normal bonds we build from parenting a child all day, every day for months and possibly years are only one factor that makes saying goodbye so difficult. As I discovered in my first placement with Kaine, it is hard to let go after you see a child healing and making progress in your home. The long-term statistics for children who have spent time in the foster care system are not good. Twenty percent become instantly homeless when they age out of the system. Only 53 percent finish high school, and less than 3 percent earn a college degree by age twenty-six. Only half find and maintain a job by age twenty-four. Sixty percent of young women who age out of the system end up in the sex industry, with 70 percent of girls becoming pregnant by age twenty-one. A quarter of all kids in foster care will end up in prison, and that number goes up to 90 percent for those with five or more foster placements.[6] As bleak as the numbers are, when we see one of our children make progress, it gives us hope that they will be able to break the mold. We begin to see just a glimpse of the future that could be.

My greatest fear is that all my child's progress will disappear, going "Poof!" when they go back to either their bio parents or a kinship placement within the same family dynamic. Who is going to help them with their homework? I have tutors for my kids to help them get on grade level in reading, math, and science, since most kids in the system are behind in school. They are behind because no one cares enough to make sure they succeed. I care. How can I let them go back?

It is also easy as a foster parent to begin to see our standard of living as the minimum our children need for the rest of their lives. I have a five-bedroom home. Each child has their own room. We always have regular meals and snacks available. In my home, every child has structure and routine. How, then, can I even think about them going back to their bio parents or to a relative who lives in a one-bedroom trailer home? I have a really nice car, and I need it to get my kids to all their appointments and school and sports. How will they get to where they need to go in a household that has a car that barely runs? I also try to protect my children's innocence in what they watch and what they are exposed to in life. Most of them are going to go back to an ugly situation, even if it is much improved from what it was before because conditions have to be better for the children to go back to their bio parents. Even then, the parents' homes rarely, if ever, measure up to the standards I have in my home.

6. Elisabeth Balistreri, "What Happens to Kids Who Age Out of Foster Care?," House of Providence, March 3, 2023, https://www.hopearmy.org/articles/what -happens-to-kids-who-age-out-of-foster-care.

How can it possibly be right to remove children from my home to send them back to that? These are all the thoughts that come to us naturally, but we cannot let them have the final word.

God has ordained the child's parents to be their parents. Who am I to say he's wrong? Does this mean I think God wants a child to go back to an abusive situation? Of course not! Jesus showed that caring for children was one of his top priorities. However, just because a family is poor does not make them unfit. Just because a parent has struggled with addiction does not mean they cannot overcome it and be a good mom or dad. Just because a family does not have my standard of living and my advantages does not disqualify them in any way. We slip into a toxic savior complex if we think otherwise.

Make no mistake about it. I find it difficult to watch one of my kids go back to a situation where I know they are going to struggle financially, emotionally, and even educationally. But it is not my responsibility to fix it. Instead, I work to build and maintain relationships with the bio parents so that I can be a resource if they need me. Believe me, I know this isn't an easy position to take. In my work with a nonprofit that took leaders from across America to different regions in other nations as a way of gaining sponsorships for poor children, I saw this same struggle all the time. I came from one of those countries and was once one of those kids. I have been with Americans on mission-type trips where we go to villages exactly like mine. So often, I hear the Americans bemoan the conditions of the people and say things like, "I wish I could gather all these kids up and take them back to America so that they'd have a chance." I understand what they mean by this. They think their statement is compassionate, but in reality it's elitist and entitled. We cannot project our own biases and assumptions onto these families in these villages, just as we cannot do the same with bio families.

"But the kids would be better off with me," you may argue. To that I say, "By what standard?"

Sure, they may have nicer clothes and a smarter phone and better food. But is that the only measure of a better life? We do our work as foster parents to help our kids not only when they are with us but also when they go back home. During the short time we have them, our job is to equip them with the skills to succeed and to give them a place to heal. Once they go back to their bio homes, they leave better off than when they came to us.

That's the role of a foster parent.

Not About Us

No matter how hard it is for us to say goodbye to a child, it is even harder for them. The pull between two worlds does not magically go away when a child is reunited with their bio family. If anything, for many, the pull becomes even worse. At least when the child lived with us, they got to see their bio parents. However, once a child leaves our home, they are gone. Our regular interaction ends. Even if we stay in touch, their feeling of betraying their bio parents by loving us becomes even stronger. They often feel guilty for missing us and their foster brothers and sisters along with missing their friends, school, and every other part of the life they'd grown accustomed to. Just as they had to start their lives over from scratch when they entered foster care, now they must do the same thing again, either with their bio parents, the relative who stepped up to take custody, or an adoptive family if we do not adopt them once parental rights are terminated. Being pulled from our homes is just one more round of trauma for children.

I've seen this play out over and over again. I've had children who talked nonstop about going home yet still broke down in tears when they had to say goodbye to me for the final time. Other kids who have stayed with me for a year, or two, or three, or even more made it clear that they did not want to leave me. They wanted to live with me forever. When a judge ruled otherwise and sent them to an aunt they could barely remember, the goodbye was the most heart-wrenching, painful experience for both of us. Several of my children have even told me that they want their mother back, but they want her to come live in my home with them as one big family. These kids want to hold on to both the families they love, but, like everything in the foster care system for a child, no one gives them a choice.

I think about all this and more every time I start to feel sorry for myself when I have to say goodbye. I signed up for this heartbreak; my children did not. The best thing I can possibly do is to try to make the transition to their new home as seamless as possible. Saying goodbye is never easy, but it is the ultimate goal for our kids. This is our calling—our responsibility.

If we do not do this, who will?

24

A Child Aging Out of the System Still Needs You

In my home village in Uganda, the passage from childhood to adulthood came at age sixteen. For boys, the journey was completed with the ritual of circumcision. From that moment, the rest of the tribe saw you as an adult—someone mature enough to tackle any challenge. Circumcision gave you a seat at the table to make decisions. No longer could you make the excuse that you were too young and too inexperienced. You had passed the test. You were now an adult who could marry, have children, and even lead the village. From the age of sixteen on, you could do or be anything.

We don't really have a similar rite of passage in the United States. The closest we have is turning eighteen. Although you must wait until you are twenty-one to drink legally, once you turn eighteen you are considered an adult capable of making adult decisions. You can buy cigarettes, play the lottery, even get a tattoo. This country even trusts eighteen-year-olds to vote on the leadership of the nation, although you have to wait another seven years to serve in the House of Representatives, twelve years to be a United States senator, and seventeen years to be an American president. In the eyes of the law, you are now an adult able to make adult decisions with adult consequences.

For children in the foster care system, their eighteenth birthday marks a major turning point they have been looking forward to since the day they landed in their first foster home. On their eighteenth birthday, they officially age out of the system. For them it feels like they're getting out of jail, which is why most of them leave our homes on their birthday. Even if they stay, listening to us is now completely optional. We can't tell them to finish high school, get a job, or even take out the trash. Well, we can, but they don't have to listen. Instead of taking out the trash they can just as easily say, "I'm out of here," and there's nothing we can do to stop it.

One of my primary jobs as a foster dad is to do everything I can to prepare my kids for this milestone so they are ready to live as fully functioning, independent, responsible adults. When they are young, I have much more influence. I teach them to make good decisions by letting them make their own choices and live with the consequences, but I set age-appropriate parameters on their choices to protect them. When I have a toddler, I let them pick out their clothes for the day, but I give them three outfits to decide between. With young children, I let them choose what they want to eat for a snack out of the ones I bought for them. With kids who are old enough for a smartphone, they can do whatever they want on their phone, but I install apps that keep them from being able to access things like porn. When one of my kids works around those apps, they lose their smartphone and must live with a flip phone. Consequences are the greatest teachers I've ever found. As my kids get older, I let them share more of the responsibility for their own lives while also letting the consequences grow. My role as Dad slowly moves to being more of a mentor, not a decision maker for them. I know the day is coming when they will be responsible for all their choices, and I do all I can for them to be ready when they get there.

Is, then, an eighteen-year-old coming out of the foster care system ready to be a fully functioning, independent, responsible adult? Is any eighteen-year-old? Of course not! But here's the reality for our foster kids: they don't care if we think they are ready. All they know is that, since the day a social worker first showed up at their home and took them away from their parents, someone else has been making all their big life decisions for them.

They didn't want to leave their moms and dads to go live with strangers, but it wasn't their choice. They didn't want to see their parents only once every one or two weeks, and then for only an hour or two at a time, but it wasn't their choice. They finally settled into the foster home and started making friends at school only to be removed from that home and told they were going to go live with an aunt they barely knew. They didn't want to move, but it wasn't their choice. When living with the aunt didn't work out, they wanted to go back to their old foster home, but they didn't get to. Instead, they ended up with another set of strangers with another new school they didn't want to go to. Again, it wasn't their choice.

These kids' lives are continually shifting up and down and back and forth, and no one ever asks them what they want to do. But they know that's going to change on the day they turn eighteen. When they hit that magic number, they make their own life decisions. Most really want to reconnect with their bio parents, so often the first thing they do is go off in search of them. Most hate school, and now they get to decide whether or not they are going to continue, and many choose not to. They're going to go where they want to go and do what they want to do, and for the first time in their lives, no one has the authority to stop them.

I try to keep all of this in mind when one of my kids leaves the day they turn eighteen. My child and I may have discussed all sorts of plans for how they are going to finish high school and what they plan to do next, but that doesn't matter as much as the pull of taking control of their own lives. The minute they have freedom to choose, all our plans go out the window.

When this happens (and it will!), foster parents can do one of three things. First, we can wash our hands of the child. After all, we did what we were supposed to do. We provided a safe place for the child to live. We took them to all the court-mandated counseling sessions, therapist appointments, and everything else required to help them heal from their trauma. We took them to school, helped with their homework, and did everything we could to set them up to graduate. If they want to throw all that away, that's their choice. We're done. They are now officially men and women and whatever other gender classification they want to put on themselves. Whatever happens from this point forward in their lives is on them. That's one option.

Option two is when the child declares they are an adult and they're going to go do what they want to do, we kick into savior mode. Savior mode means we do everything within our power to keep our child safe from themselves. One of my first kids to age out of the system left my house as soon as they turned eighteen to go off in search of their birth parents. They found them, and it did not go well. The bio parent kicked them out. They called, asking to move back into my house. Savior mode told me to say, "Of course!" But I said no. You may think that sounds horrible, but I did it because I wanted the child to live with the consequences of their decision. I had tried to talk them into waiting just a few months, until they graduated from high school, but they still left. When that decision blew up in their face, they wanted to come back.

I have had many children come back to my home after their reunification with their bio parents resulted in them being thrown back into the foster care system, but this eighteen-year-old was not in the system. They had left, and as far as I knew they'd turn around and leave again the moment I disagreed with one of their life choices. That's why I said no. They wanted to be treated like an adult, which is exactly what I was doing.

I did not hear from my now-adult child for three or four months after that. I didn't try to chase them down. In the story of the prodigal son in the Bible, the father does not chase after his adult son, and neither did I. However, just as the prodigal son eventually came back and the father welcomed him, when my child called, I was there for them. And that is our third option: when a child in our care ages out of the system and declares their independence, we maintain our relationship and stay as close as a phone call.

I stayed available for my child to call whenever they needed. Eventually my child did call. They wanted to come back, not to live but just to visit. When they asked me about going back to finish high school, I encouraged their decision. After they graduated, they asked if they could stay with me temporarily as they worked and saved money to get an apartment. This time, I said yes. I also put a timetable on how long they could stay and what they'd have to do to show progress toward their goal.

The relationship we had after they moved back in as an adult was very different. One day they called me from work. They had forgotten to charge their electric scooter the night before, and now it had died and they could not get home. "Can you come pick me up?" they asked. You can probably guess my answer. Without me stepping in, they figured out a way to get back to my house. From that point forward, the scooter was always plugged in at night. My adult child was not thrilled that I left them to figure it out on their own, but they also weren't surprised. After all, I tell all my older children that if they are ever arrested, I will not bail them out of jail. Instead I will come and visit them in jail every day. In other words, don't break the law, because if you do, it's on you, but I will be here for you.

A Family Support System

Children who age out do not always call back. When they do, that shows they have no one else to turn to, which goes to the heart of the reason our work with a child does not end when they age out of the system. A child who grows up in the foster care system may think of themselves as an adult when they turn eighteen, but no eighteen-year-old is ready for the level of independence a former foster kid has. A child who ages out of the system does not have any sort of family support system behind them. I am not talking about financial support, either. When any young adult goes out into the real world, they face all sorts of obstacles that are difficult to figure out on their own. For example, a child who wants to go to college or trade school has to first fill out the federal financial aid form known as the FAFSA. It is a long and confusing form. Most children with loving and supportive families get help from their parents with the form, or, in most cases, the parent fills it out for them. A young adult who has aged out of the foster care system is on their own. Perhaps that is part of the reason why so few ever go to or finish college. All of the forms that must be filled out can be overwhelming.

If the young adult decides to go get a job instead, they still have questions to answer and forms to fill out, like the W-4. Getting insurance and renting an apartment and filing taxes and all the other "adult" activities waiting for them are equally overwhelming. Without a parent to call for answers, where are these kids going to turn? Who will help them navigate buying a car or even getting a driver's license? And that's just the start of life. Remember the statistics: 70 percent of all young women who age out of the system will be pregnant by age twenty-one. Nothing makes a young woman turn to her mother for help like having a baby. First-time soon-to-be moms have millions of questions about what to expect. Once the baby comes, they have a million more. Again, where are they supposed to turn, if not to us?

When a child ages out of the system, they are on their own, but we can make sure they are not alone. We must give them the independence they crave—as if we had a choice. The statistics for kids aging out of the system are so bad because so few of these young adults have someone to whom they can turn for answers and for support, someone who loves them no matter what. But if we do our job right leading up to that day, they will know we remain that mom or dad they can turn to for the kind of loving support only a family can give. Providing a family support system after children age out of foster care is crucial if we ever hope to break the foster care cycle.

25

Embrace Social Workers and Teachers as Partners in This Journey

My phone rings in the middle of the night. With the exception of my family in Uganda who don't always remember the seven-hour difference between us, there's only one reason my phone rings in the middle of the night.

"Peter, this is Julie," the social worker from the agency I work through says as I answer. "I have a pair of siblings that need a home right now. The boy is five, and his little sister is three. Can you take them?"

"Possibly," I say.

"I tell you what. I'll give you ten minutes to think about it. Will that work?"

"Sure," I reply.

Ten minutes later, Julie calls back for my answer, which is yes. A few minutes after that, a social worker from the county calls. I don't recognize her name, even though I thought I've met most of the social workers in my county. She's probably new. The turnover rate for her profession is very high.

Twenty minutes later I meet the county worker in a Walmart parking lot for what feels like a clandestine exchange. I learn the children's names as I put them in car seats. The social worker thanks me as she hands me a bag that contains one set of clothes for each child, a couple of toddler-sized diapers for the little girl, and the little boy's medication. She tells me everything she knows about the kids (which, as usual, is not much at all). She first met them an hour or so earlier when the police called her to pick up the kids from their home because the mom was being arrested on drug and prostitution charges. Before I leave, she says something about how this is the third night this week she's been called out for an emergency placement. I shake my head and whisper to her how sorry I am. I feel her pain. Still, deep down I know that no matter how hard my days may be as a foster dad, I'd never, ever want to trade places with her.

Social Workers Are Not the Enemy

Being a foster parent is tough, but a social worker's job is impossible. I think all of us as foster parents know this is true, but that doesn't stop us from complaining about the social worker who failed to inform us that the six-year-old we just picked up is on the autism spectrum. "If I'd known this," we mutter to ourselves, "I would have said no. I'm not able to handle them plus the three other kids in my house." But usually the social worker didn't tell us because they simply didn't know themselves.

Or we get angry because they didn't inform us of all the behavioral issues the twelve-year-old who has bounced from foster home to foster home over the last six years has. We're home number eight. "She should have told me," we complain, "but I bet she didn't because that's the only way she could get anyone to take them." Which is probably true. And yet the child still needed a home. Sleeping at the county social services office isn't really an option for any child. If we were in the social worker's shoes, what would we do?

We also get annoyed when our phone calls to our social workers aren't answered quickly or when it seems like the social worker barely has time for us. It seems that way because they don't. Most are underpaid and overworked. Turnover is very high. I don't know how they do what they do.

The worst is when we get mad at the social worker when a placement turns difficult, which, as you can tell from reading this book, happens all the time. "How was I supposed to know this child would lie to my face? I can't trust them. How am I supposed to parent them?" we complain. Yet we are told from the very beginning in our training classes that this is exactly what we should expect. The lying, the stealing, the broken trust, the manipulation, even the poop on the bathroom walls are all things about which we were warned before we ever got our foster care license and received our first placement. Hearing about it in a class and actually experiencing it are two very different things. We feel blindsided and become angry, but we shouldn't be. The social workers who trained us and trusted us enough to place a child in our care told us what to expect. We can't blame them when those very things happen.

The anger a lot of foster parents throw on the social workers is nothing compared to what social workers get on the other side. As foster parents, we deal with our children's trauma. The stories our kids tell us when they finally open up break our hearts. Social workers see these horror stories lived out every single day. Only when they step in, they are the bad guys. A bio parent can be an abusive drug lord, but the social worker who removes the child from the situation becomes the embodiment of evil in the eyes of the child who doesn't understand why they can't stay with their parent. "That woman forced her way in and stole my child," a mom will say, forgetting to add that she was in the process of being arrested and sent to jail for a very long time. Often these parents are violent people, which means the social workers are literally putting themselves and their families at risk just by doing their jobs.

Social workers also catch the blame when bio parents stay locked in the behaviors that caused their children to be removed in the first place, and therefore the kids don't get to go back to them. "I did everything I could to get you back, but that man didn't care," a bio parent will complain on the phone to a child. Of course this is a lie, but the child doesn't know it.

Instead of seeing the social workers who make the foster care system function as the enemy, I choose to see them for what they are: a part of my parenting team. If not for them, I would not have my children. They trained me. They entrusted these children's care to me. They follow up and receive regular reports back from me on the kids. I want to honor that, which is why I try to balance my reports about my children. Most of us usually only call the DCS office when we have a problem with one of our foster kids. As a result, all they hear from us are the bad things our kids have done, like we're giving them a police rap sheet. No one calls because a kid got an A on a report card or scored a goal in a soccer game. I try to break the mold and give reports of the good as well as the bad. Whenever I have a small victory with one of my kids, I want to share it with the social worker on the case so that they can know progress has been made. In a job that sees the worst in humanity daily, I want to help them see that their efforts do bear fruit.

Teachers Play a Key Role

For nine months out of the year, my school-age children spend more time at school than they do at home. As a result, my kids are with their teachers more than they are with me. This also means that the teachers must endure my kids doing to them the same things they do at home to me.

Do I mean to imply that my child will lie to a teacher? Absolutely.

Will they steal? Of course.

Will they be disruptive? Guaranteed.

Will they be clingy and fall apart if the teacher leaves the room? Yes.

Will they do things that seem completely abnormal to the teacher and the rest of the class but are completely normal to the child? What do you think?

While children may well act out more at home than at school because they feel safer at home, our kids cannot keep a lid on all that is bubbling up inside of them forever. Eventually, it will come out at school, and when it does, our phones will ring. I learned this truth the first day my first placement, Kaine, went to school. Many of our kids will become very, very acquainted with seeing the principal and getting suspended from school. We should expect it.

Shouldn't we hope for the best with our kids? Of course. But hoping for the best doesn't mean shutting our eyes to reality, and the reality is that kids from hard places act out at school. Not only do we need to be prepared when it happens, but we should also help prepare the teachers and administrators in the school to deal with our child's behavior.

Because of privacy laws, we obviously cannot share everything about our child's situation. However, we can team up with the teachers and help them understand the warning signs that a meltdown is on its way. We should also meet with them and help them recognize the triggers that can set our child off before they find themselves trying to stop our kid from flipping over tables and chairs. Teachers want our kids to succeed. We want our kids to succeed. Working together is the best way to make that happen.

I also think it is important to establish a good relationship with each of my kids' teachers. I have had teachers tell me that when a child gets in trouble, many parents march up to the school and immediately blame the teacher. Having a mom or dad do just the opposite is refreshing. As foster parents, we hold no illusions that our kids are little angels. Every parent should have this point of view. I know teachers are not perfect, but I also know how difficult their job is. That is why, whenever one of my kids gets in serious enough trouble that I get called to the school for a parent/teacher meeting, I always bring the teacher a coffee. Of course, my kids hate it when I do that.

"Dad, she was so mean to me," they cry. "How can you buy her coffee?"

I always smile, because I know that the teacher was "mean" because, for example, my child kicked her as hard as he could. A coffee is not just a little peace offering on my part. It is also my way of showing the teacher that I get it. I understand my child's behavior at school because I see it at home. I appreciate their patience with my child as we work through this together. Does this mean I always believe the teacher over my child? No. But I try to give the teacher the benefit of the doubt because I know my child's success often hinges on what happens in that classroom.

I am also especially grateful to the teachers when I don't hear from them for a week or two. I praise the Lord for that! When I go in for a regular parent/teacher conference, I celebrate these small wins with the teacher. They are part of this team with me. Most teachers my kids have had are very special people, and I am grateful for them.

Teachers and parents are on the same side. Embrace them. Encourage them. And take them a coffee when your child turns over every table in the room because they didn't get to finish an art project.

EPILOGUE

No Matter Where You Are in This Journey, There Is Hope

Before I became a dad, I traveled all over the world with a major international child advocacy organization. Over the span of a decade, I made between two and three hundred trips to Asia, Africa, and South America as I took major donors and influencers to see at-risk children up close. When I wasn't flying around the world, I was flying from coast to coast here in the United States. I flew anywhere and everywhere, speaking in churches, at conferences, in corporate settings, and anywhere else we could get people together to hear about sponsoring children. I spent so little time at home in Colorado that I should have had my mail sent to an airport because that was more of a home address to me. I lived in the air.

I still have the same basic job, but with a different organization and a different job description. I no longer travel around the world regularly, although I will make a trip from time to time. Most of my work involves speaking in the US, and even then I try to limit any travel to the weekends. Over the course of my career I've raised millions of dollars for kids around the world. I used to think my work as a child advocate was my way of paying it forward for the kindness of a stranger who changed my life. Not any longer.

If you've read my first book, you know how I met a foster dad named Jason on one of my international trips. Jason was also a pastor in Texas. Over the course of our ten days together, he explained both the incredible need for foster parents and the joys it can bring. I don't remember if we talked about the challenges on which I've focused in this book. Before my conversations with Jason, I thought I was doing all I could do for children whose childhoods resembled mine. But by the time I got back to Denver after that trip, I knew I had to do something else. That's when I started on my own parental journey. My only regret is that I did not start earlier in life.

However, there is one little detail about my own story I did not include in my first book. Perhaps I should have shared this detail in the opening chapter of this book, but I thought it best to save it for now if I actually wanted people to read past page 1. After all, what kind of father admits that, before I had children, I avoided kids as much as possible? Every time I went into a restaurant, I scanned the room to see where the children might be so that I could be seated as far from them as possible. If I noticed lots of families with young children, I usually turned around and went somewhere else. As someone who'd never had kids, all I ever really noticed were kids acting out. I always felt sorry for the mom or dad frantically trying to calm a child. *I'm glad that's not me*, I usually thought.

It wasn't just restaurants where I avoided kids. When I flew, if I found myself seated in the same row as a mom or dad with a small child, I always asked to be moved at least five or six rows away from them. From time to time I went so far as to pay extra to be moved into first class rather than have to sit through a flight with a child crying or whining or throwing a fit. Here I was, flying all over the world advocating for children, but I did not want to spend four hours or more on a flight near one who was crying or screaming or fidgeting or doing any of the things that are now pretty much my everyday life. I loved kids—but from afar. I wanted to make a difference in the lives of children—but always from a safe distance. I spoke to thousands at a time about the need to step up and help children have better lives—but I also spent thousands to give myself a better seat on a plane rather than sit next to one. Looking back, I can't see that guy ever reading a book like this, much less writing one.

But I am not that child-avoiding guy any longer. I am a dad. I shared this dark secret about myself to let you know that if someone like me can be an effective parent, so can you. No matter where you are in your parenting journey, there is hope. You can make a difference in the lives of your children whether they come into your home through birth or the foster care system or adoption. We all have days where we are certain we're the least qualified person on the planet to be entrusted with a family. Believe me, I feel like that nearly every day. But then my child calls me Dad, and I know God has me here for a reason.

As parents, we have very little control over the outcomes in our children's lives. All we can do is our best, and our best is enough. More than anything, the best thing we can give our children is to love them as God loves us. At times we will experience heartache as our kids react to our love the same way we often do to God's. Don't give up. Hang in there. You are the one God has chosen to parent your children. He knows you are up to it.

PETER MUTABAZI is an entrepreneur, an international advocate for children, and the founder of Now I Am Known, a nonprofit that supplies resources that encourage and affirm children and families. A single adoptive father of three (and counting) and foster dad to many, Mutabazi is a former street kid who has worked for World Vision, Com-  passion International, and the Red Cross, and has appeared on media outlets such as the BBC, CNN, *USA Today*, and *The TODAY Show*. A passionate and popular speaker, he currently lives in Charlotte, North Carolina.

CONNECT WITH PETER:

NowIAmKnown.org

@PeterMutabaziFosterDad

@FosterDadFlipper

@FosterDadFlippr

@NowIAmKnown

@NowIAmKnown